BROKEN-DOWN
HOUSE

BROKEN-DOWN
HOUSE

Living Productively in a World Gone Bad

Paul David Tripp

Shepherd Press
Wapwallopen, Pennsylvania

ISBN: 978-0-9815400-6-1
Published by Shepherd Press
P.O. Box 24
Wapwallopen, Pennsylvania 18660

Page design and typesetting by Lakeside Design Plus
Cover design by Tobias' Outerwear for Books

First Printing, 2009
Printed in the United States of America

PAH   20   19   18   17   16   15   14   13
14   13   12   11   10   9   8   7   6   5

Thanks, Steve,
I couldn't have done it without you.

Contents

Preface

The Bible is a picture book in many ways. No, God didn't include drawings or photographs for you, but the language of the Bible is wonderfully visual and graphic. Again and again, God reaches into the physical world and paints a familiar image to help us grasp the less familiar realities of the spiritual world. Bread, the sun, a rock, a river, a judge, a flower, a lion, and more all become visual tools for understanding God and his kingdom. It is not an accident that the physical world pictures the spiritual world so well. This was part of God's intention. He embedded rich metaphors all over the universe he made, knowing full well that he would employ them to help us understand the spiritual realities we must grasp in order to live life his way.

The more I study Scripture, the more I appreciate this quality of vibrant physicality. Word pictures splash across page after page, reminding us how much God cares for us. From the seed in the ground, to the cross to be carried, to the weed, to the treasure in the field, God wants to draw from his storehouse of physical examples to help us know him, ourselves, and our world more accurately. This means that, in simply looking out my window, I can be reminded of precious truths that God has connected to the physical world I am viewing.

This book is written around one modern word picture, the broken-down house. We've all seen them—those sagging and dilapidated dwellings that look as if they are in physical pain. As you pass by, you wonder what the house once looked like, who lived in it, and how it got into such a miserable condition. Some of us look at this kind of house and are simply overwhelmed. We quickly move on, not for a moment considering the possibility of restoration. Others of us immediately see potential. We can't wait to get our hands on the mess and restore it to its former beauty.

Well, sin has ravaged the beautiful house that God created. This world bears only the faintest resemblance to what it was built to be. It sits slumped, disheveled, in pain, groaning for the restoration that can only be accomplished by the hands of him who built it in the first place. The Bible clearly tells us that the divine Builder cannot and will not leave his house in its present pitiful condition. He has instituted a plan of restoration, and he will not relent until everything about his house is made totally new again. That is the good news.

The bad news is that you and I are living right in the middle of the restoration. We live each day in a house that is terribly broken, where nothing works exactly as intended. But we do not live in the house by ourselves. Emmanuel lives here as well, and he is at work returning his house to its former beauty. Often it doesn't look like any real restoration is going on at all. Things seem to get messier, uglier, and less functional all the time. But that's the way it is with restoration; things generally get worse before they get better.

So in the pages that follow, I invite you to consider one simple thing. What does it look like to live productively in a world—a "house"—that is broken down? Someday you will live forever in a fully restored house. But right now you are called to live with peace, joy, and productivity in a place that has been sadly damaged by sin. How can you live above the damage? Even better, how can you be an active part of the restoration that is at the heart of God's plan of redemption? This is what the book you have in your hands is all about.

May God help you to be fruitful in all you do, even though you live in a broken-down house!

Paul David Tripp

7/21/08

PART ONE

Knowing

Broken-Down House

Shards of window glass
shimmer
in
weed-strewn sod.
Roof shingles
clap
with the wind,
a spontaneous ovation
for
the dwelling
that once was.
With creaking voices
dark halls
repeat
long-gone conversations.
Too much
decay
too much
damage
violent elements
have disrespected
the carpenter's
dream.
The sagging-porch frown
tells a painful story
of beauty shattered.
All that's left
is a
broken-down house.

Life in This Broken-Down House

I really did think he had lost his mind. I couldn't believe he was going to do what he was about to do. I tried to reason with him, but he was so excited and engaged, I don't think he heard a word I said.

The day had started out normally. We were with Luella's parents having a leisurely breakfast and discussing whether we wanted to venture out into the Florida sun, when my father-in-law chimed in that he would like to go look at houses. My mother-in-law was not interested at all. The thought of getting out of the car again and again in the blazing sun to tour house after house held no attraction for her. So he extended the invitation to me, and I agreed to go.

He had done his research well and knew of several houses he wanted to see. One particular house was at the top of his list, so we drove to the north side of Miami and into a rundown neighborhood. Already I was thinking, *Why would he want to own a house here?* I hadn't seen anything yet. As we wove our way through the ribbon streets we came upon a lot that could have passed as a bomb site. That's when my father-in-law stopped the car.

The first thing that hit me was the condition of the front yard. The grass was beyond cutting; it needed harvesting. Scattered across this suburban savanna was a random collection of rotting mechanical debris. Old lawnmowers, decrepit appliances, and rusting car parts were strewn everywhere. The house had at one time been painted white, I think. But time, sun, dirt, wind, and neglect had given it a sickly, grayish-yellow skin, mottled and peeling everywhere. The storm door hung at an odd slant, held in place by one rusty hinge.

While I was still trying to take it all in, my father-in-law turned to me and said cheerfully, "Well, this looks promising!" I checked in every direction, trying to identify anything that might fit his description. *Promising? What, exactly, seems promising here?* When he followed up with, "Let's go in and take a look," I began to wonder if he was delusional. A strong desire to protect this man from himself rose up in me. It didn't seem possible that he could be seeing what I was seeing and still use the word *promising*.

We walked up the grease-stained driveway to the tottering front door and my father-in-law gave it a good knock. I half expected the house to collapse in front of us. An older man, as dirty and unkempt as his surroundings, invited us in. I remember thinking he was just the kind of man you would expect to live in such a place.

The inside of the house actually made the outside look pretty good. As I glanced about me, there seemed to be nothing that was clean and whole. Every inch appeared stained and dirty. Every corner seemed filled with junk. Every feature of the house looked to be damaged in some way. It was overwhelming. As we sat on a filthy, sagging couch in the middle of this broken-down house, that puzzling sentence kept echoing through my mind . . . *Well, this looks promising!* Emerging from my daze, I realized my father-in-law had actually begun to negotiate for the house. I wanted to stop him, but I couldn't. He was too focused and excited.

Within a few days my father-in-law had secured the money to buy the house. Not long afterward, he moved in and began a complete and total restoration. I will never forget walking into that house after all the work had been completed. It was hard to imagine it was the same house.

This Broken-Down World

The world you live in is a lot like that broken-down house. Every single room has been dirtied and damaged by sin. Not one part of it shines with anything like the pure glory that was so evident when it was first made. Sin has left this world in a sorry condition. You see it everywhere you look.

You see it in great cities and small communities. You see it in the environment, blighted by pollution and misuse. You see it in government, often focused more on caring for itself than on serving the people. You see it in entertainment that replaces what is truly beautiful with what is essentially pornography. You see it in the family, as the place designed for growth and protection often becomes a source of life's greatest hurts. You see it in a staggering, diseased economy that has finally exhausted itself after decades of financial debauchery. You see it in art and culture that often debases the very concept of beauty. You see it in history, with instance after instance of man's inhumanity to man. You see it in each life as we all struggle with physical, emotional, spiritual, and relational brokenness every day.

The brokenness around you affects you in different ways at different times. Sometimes you have to deal with personal hurt. Sometimes you grow angry that things do not function as they were designed to. Sometimes you are overwhelmed with feeling sad or lost in the face of this world's pitiful condition. Sometimes you get tired of the effort it takes to live in a broken-down house, and you just want to quit. At every point and every moment, your life is messier and more complicated than it really ought to be because everything is so much more difficult in such a terribly broken world.

But let us also see that this world of ours is *more* than a broken-down house. It is a broken-down house in the process of being restored.

There's a Whole Lot of Restoration Going On

Like my father-in-law examining that ruined little house in Miami, God is not willing for this broken-down world to stay in its sorry condition. As Creator, he is able to look at it and see promise, the promise of a total restoration of its beauty. And he has asked you to move in with him to be one of his tools of restoration.

While it is hard to live in a house that needs to be restored, in some ways it is even harder to live there while the restoration takes place. Not only is everything more difficult in a broken house, there is also the dust and dirt of restoration and the intermittent noise and chaos and sweat and soreness that comes with the repairs. Try as you may to keep the dust sealed off in one room, you find grit in the drawers and on your food. The din of creative destruction wears you down. The labor wears you out.

There are days when you simply don't want to face it. Other days, you forget the mess you're living in for a moment, only to step on a rusty nail or through a rotted step. You often find yourself dreaming of what it would be like to live in a house that needed no restoration, and you wonder if the job will ever be completed. You want to hold on to the promise of everything eventually being fixed, but it's hard. You want to rest, but there's work to do. You want to escape, but you can't—this is your house and you have to live in it. You wonder if what you are seeing is really progress. In fact, it often seems like you're losing ground. The kitchen is more usable than it was, and the pipes from the upstairs bathtub don't drench the living room anymore. But now the staircase has been ripped out and the only way to your bedroom is by a ladder! In light of this mess and all the work yet to be done, it is difficult to celebrate progress for very long. You have worked hard, but so much restoration is still needed.

This interwoven set of difficulties is the environment you live in every day. It is the only environment you have. It conditions what you face as an individual. It shapes what you experience in your family. It structures the struggles of your marriage and friendships. It creates the stresses of your community. It determines the issues that politicians and government officials must deal with. It molds the work of the church. It affects the condition of the physical environment. It shapes the struggles of your heart and mind. It even determines the things you deal with in your body.

The fact that you live in a broken-down house in the midst of restoration makes everything more difficult. It removes the ease and simplicity of life. It requires you to be more thoughtful, more careful. It requires you to listen and see well. It requires you to look out for difficulty and to be aware of danger. It requires you to contemplate and plan. It requires you to do what you don't really want to do and to accept what you find difficult to accept. You want to simply coast, but you can't. Things are broken and they need to be fixed. There is work to do.

You can tell if a house is being condemned or restored by the size of the tools that are in use. If there's a crane equipped with a wrecking ball out front, you can give up on restoration. But if there are a lot of hand tools around, that's a sign of hope. True restoration takes patience, subtlety, skill, and grace. I live in Philadelphia where a lot of restoration goes on. I once wandered into a row house that was being lovingly restored. In the high-ceilinged living room I found a man on scaffolding removing antique moldings. It was triple-crown molding—three separate moldings fitted together to create a beautiful effect. He wasn't trying to pry off the molding with a big crowbar because he knew that would splinter and break it. He was using a very small hammer to drive very small wedges between the molding and the wall. It was a tedious job, requiring much patience, but he did it because he had restoration in mind, not destruction. Across the room were three piles of molding he had already removed, every piece perfectly intact. That molding would be refinished and hang on the wall in beauty once again.

Living Productively in a Broken-Down House

So, that's what this book is about. What does it look like on a practical level to live well in a broken-down world that is being restored? What does it look like to live a restoration lifestyle—to live productively in a broken place? What does it look like to function as one of God's tools of restoration?

This book proposes that you have been created and called by God for more than survival. You have been created and called to care for more than just yourself. You have been chosen to be engaged in a process—to care about, to work for, and to embrace the promise and possibility of a restoration lifestyle.

The reason the old man's house had gotten so bad is that he didn't care. He was willing to settle for personal survival. He didn't live with hope or promise. He lived a life of avoidance and daily denial. He wouldn't let himself face how bad it was and how good it could be. He didn't care what the house looked like to his neighbors and he didn't seem to mind that it was getting worse. He gave in as the house gave out, so things just got worse and worse.

But God does care, and he calls you to care. God is not satisfied with the state of this house, and he calls us to share in his holy dissatisfaction. In our hearts he wants dissatisfaction and hope to kiss. He wants us, every day that we live, to embrace the gospel promise of a world made new. He wants our lives to be shaped by uncompromising honesty and undiminished hope. He wants us to face how bad things really are, not as survivalists, but as restorers. He wants to pick us up in his hands and use us as the hammers, saws, and screwdrivers of a brand new world. He wants us to believe that because of what he has done there is hope for new beginnings and fresh starts.

Your Lord is the ultimate Restorer, and he never rests. One day his work will be over and the world will be completely renewed. In the meantime, he calls you and me to live in this broken-down house with hearts of patience and eyes of promise. He calls us away from self-focused survival and to the hard work of restoration. He calls us away from paralyzing discouragement and the nagging desire to quit. He welcomes us to live in the patience and grace that only he can give.

God calls us to live productively in a world gone bad. Do you understand what that means?

A Light in His Hands

So little preparation
so many
unrealistic expectations
so often
dreams are dashed
unwanted fears
realized.
Too few
understand where they are
too few
know where they're going
too many
feel alone and lost.
Yet the One who knows
and who understands
has joined the journey.
He holds a light
in His hands
and He is One
who can be trusted.

2

Know Where You Are

*L*et me ask what may seem like a stupid question.

Do you know where you live? No, I don't mean your street address. I want you to see the most deeply spiritual and profoundly personal implications of this question.

Do you bring to each day the realistic expectations that come from a cogent understanding of your life, yourself, and your world? Still confused? Then let's break it down a little.

Is there anything that is disappointing you right now? Is there a relationship or situation that is leaving you hurt and confused? Are there personal problems that you simply have not been able to solve? Do you ever feel alienated, alone, or misunderstood? Have you had to deal with mistreatment or injustice lately? Have you been hurt, angry, fearful, or discouraged? Is there any place in your life where you feel like giving up or giving in? Does your life ever seem much more complicated than it should be? Does it seem like you are always having to deal with obstacles of one kind or another?

Do you wish you didn't have so many problems on your plate? Does it bug you that even the easy things in life don't turn out to be nearly as easy as you thought they would be?

Are there problems in your past that still haunt you? Do you regularly face difficulties you have sought to solve, but which still lie open and festering? Have you ever envied someone else's life? Have you ever wished you could start over in some area of life, but you know you can't? Have you ever felt too weak and too unqualified to deal with what is confronting you? Does your life seem to move too fast for you ever to be able to catch up? Has there ever been a day in your life that was fundamentally problem-free?

When you actually spell them out, most of these questions—and maybe all of them—can find resonance in each of us. But we don't reflect on many of them very often, do we? We don't incorporate them as conscious realities into daily life. I guess we all get so used to the hardships of life in a broken world that we just quit paying attention. Besides, it's easier that way.

It's like what happens to some of us when the car begins to break down. At first your mechanically untrained ears are assaulted by a sound the car has never before made. This unearthly screech elicits fear in your mind and dismay in your heart. But for reasons you don't understand the car continues to run. For the first few days the screech drives you crazy and it seems like you're praying your way from one destination to the next. Then you begin to think the car may run much longer than you had first expected. So you cope by playing the radio loud enough to mask the noise. Before long you don't even have to do that. Your ears have become so accustomed to the screech that you don't hear it anymore. You no longer drive around fearing the imminent demise of your vehicle. You have completely forgotten that your car is in a state of terminal mechanical distress. So you are shocked when one morning it simply refuses to start.

I am convinced this is exactly what happens to us. We are confronted every day with the sights and sounds of a world in distress—our world. These things should assault our eyes and ears. Instead, they have become the familiar backgrounds and ambient noises of our daily lives. They have become so "normal" that we simply no longer hear and no longer see. The result? We no longer pay attention.

Location Amnesia and Unrealistic Expectations

I think many of us live in a permanent state of *location amnesia*. We have forgotten where we live. Lose sight of the fact that this is a broken-down house where nothing works quite right, and it sets you up for all kinds of trouble. Let me give you a prime example: marriage. There can be little question that one of the major difficulties married couples deal with is unrealistic expectations that spring from a shared case of location amnesia.

Now, part of the problem is the creepiness of the dating practices in our western culture. Honestly, most dating is only about half a step up from used-car sales. Stay with me here! To put it bluntly but accurately, the idea in Western culture dating is to sell yourself. The last thing you want is for the other person to really get to know you. Consequently, a man who doesn't like to shop will suddenly be saying things like, "Sure, honey, I would love to go to another twelve stores to look for those special shoes you have in mind." A woman who doesn't appreciate sports will find herself volunteering to watch sports with her date and his buddies for hour upon endless, grueling hour.

Having presented one another with only their best behavior, the man and woman each convince themselves that they have found a nearly perfect person. As they move toward that day when they will actually begin living together in the world's most comprehensive relationship, they do not factor into their expectations the difficulties of life in this broken-down house of a world. Then, when the marriage takes an unexpected turn they are shocked, saddened, and utterly unprepared. Six months after the wedding, the wife is crying and saying, "This is not the man I married!" But of course, he is. He is precisely the man she married. It's the guy she dated who was the fake!

The problem is that the marriage began with unrealistic expectations, a product of location amnesia. We find location amnesia at work everywhere in our lives. That job you were so jazzed about hasn't turned out to be as great as you had hoped. That church you were convinced was one of the best in the country turned out to have many of the same flaws as your previous church. You were so excited to move into that new house, only to discover that not everything was designed or built as well as it seemed. That perfect vacation was anything but perfect. Your new friend seemed so great until his inadequacies, flaws, and weaknesses showed up. That highly recommended restaurant had a waiter who was arrogant and rude. That lawn you paid so much for is now laced with weeds. Those wrinkle-free khakis do, in fact, wrinkle! We live as flawed people in a fallen world. There simply is no escaping it.

Harsh Words, Harsh Reality

I am more and more persuaded that when we characterize the Bible as a book about spirituality, we do it and ourselves a disservice. The Bible is not a higher-plane tome about some mystical life of spiritual devotion. It does not teach blissful separation from the brokenness of everyday life. No, the Bible is a book about *this* world. It is a gritty, honest book. When we read Scripture, we face the world as it actually is, in big-screen, high-def detail. God doesn't pull any punches. He doesn't paint over any cracks. He doesn't flatter or avoid. There is no denial of what is real and true.

The sights and sounds of the Bible are familiar. They are the sights and sounds of the very same broken world you and I wake up to every day. Dirt and smoke are on every page. You can't read very far without your nostrils and eyes being assaulted by the acrid air of a world gone bad. Let's be straight here, the world of the Bible stinks in many ways. Does it bother you when you read that? Does it come across to you as displaying a lack of faith? Let's look at how the Bible portrays the place where you and I live.

Sometimes the Bible's honesty about our situation comes through diagnostic observations. A good diagnosis tells you what's wrong, and the Bible accurately diagnoses the human condition on page after page. For example, the words of Genesis 6:5 tell us that, "The Lord saw how great man's wickedness on the earth had become, and that every inclination of the thoughts of his heart was only evil all the time." The words of Romans 3:10–18 are much the same,

> As it is written:
>> "There is no one righteous, not even one;
>>> there is no one who understands,
>>> no one who seeks God.
>> All have turned away,
>>> they have together become worthless;
>>> there is no one who does good,
>>> not even one."
>> "Their throats are open graves;
>>> their tongues practice deceit."
>> "The poison of vipers is on their lips."
>> "Their mouths are full of cursing and bitterness."
>> "Their feet are swift to shed blood;
>>> ruin and misery mark their ways,
>>> and the way of peace they do not know."
>> "There is no fear of God before their eyes."

Or you have the words of Romans 8:18–23 that warn us of the world we all live in every day,

> I consider that our present sufferings are not worth comparing with the glory that will be revealed in us. The creation waits in eager expectation for the sons of God to be revealed. For the creation was subjected to frustration, not by its own

choice, but by the will of the one who subjected it, in hope that the creation itself will be liberated from its bondage to decay and brought into the glorious freedom of the children of God.

We know that the whole creation has been groaning as in the pains of childbirth right up to the present time. Not only so, but we ourselves, who have the first fruits of the Spirit, groan inwardly as we wait eagerly for our adoption as sons, the redemption of our bodies.

Or you have the diagnostic description of Ephesians 6:12:

"For our struggle is not against flesh and blood, but against the rulers, against the authorities, against the powers of this dark world and against the spiritual forces of evil in the heavenly realms."

Great wickedness . . . only evil . . . no one who understands . . . worthless . . . open graves . . . deceit . . . poison . . . cursing and bitterness . . . swift to shed blood . . . ruin and misery . . . no fear of God . . . subjected to frustration . . . bondage to decay . . . groaning . . . struggle . . . this dark world . . . evil. Perhaps you are so familiar with these verses that it is difficult to see their unflinching realism. But each of these passages is honest about what you and I will encounter as we live in a world that is not operating as it was designed to operate.

The Bible is not only honest in its diagnostic observations, but in graphic, real-life, fallen-world stories as well. You have the shocking account of sibling homicide in Genesis 4, the favorite-son trickery of Rebekah in Genesis 27, and the sibling rivalry in Jacob's dysfunctional family. You have the dark idolatry of duplicitous Israel so powerfully confronted by the prophets, and the sex, power, and money intrigues of the Kings and Chronicles. The New Testament hits you with the horror of politically motivated infanticide by Herod, the sexually motivated beheading of John, and the perverted justice that leads to the crucifixion of the Messiah.

The history of your Bible drips with the blood of violence. It smells of the stench of human greed, betrayal, and perversion. It is stained with instance after instance of people on the one hand forgetting God, while on the other hand doing their best to take his place. Apart from Christ, none of the people in these stories are moral heroes who always get it right. No, to a person they are flawed. Abraham (the father of the faithful!) forces his servant girl to have sex with him because he is too impatient to wait any longer for the promised heir. David (the man after God's own heart!) is so dissatisfied with the glories and vast privileges God has given him that he takes another man's wife. Then he ends any competition for her by sending her husband to the front lines to die. Peter (a leader among the Twelve!) declares he will follow Jesus anywhere, but soon thereafter, when the public heat is on, he denies with angry curses any knowledge of the Savior.

In both its diagnoses and its descriptions, the Bible is honest about life in a fallen world. This honesty is a sign of God's love. He is the wise and gentle father preparing his child for that walk through a tough neighborhood on the first day of school. He is the faithful friend praying with you before you face an unusual challenge. He is the caring physician informing you of what to expect from the disease he has just diagnosed.

A primary goal of all this diagnosis, description, warning, comfort, and counsel is to call us to certain ways of living. Why would you need to be "completely humble and gentle; be patient, bearing with one another in love," (Ephesians 4:2–3) if you were not living in a community of flawed people where this kind of character is essential? Relationships in a fallen world are hard. Ministry to flawed people is fraught with difficulty. Character is needed because the world is broken.

In being honest, the Bible welcomes you to be honest as well. In its refusal to minimize, diminish, or deny the harsh realities of this broken-down house, the Bible calls us to face the facts as well. Things are not okay around us or inside us. The brokenness presses in on every side.

What should we do with all this? Let me suggest five ways to pursue the character qualities to which God calls us, and in that way prepare ourselves to participate more effectively in the great task of restoration.

Determine to be honest. Do not permit yourself to give way to location amnesia. Look the real world squarely in the face. Locate those places in your life where things are not the way they were meant to be and determine, by God's help, to be a reconciler and a restorer.

Let yourself mourn. If we are honest and look the world in the face, we will be sad at what we see. Jesus said, "Blessed are those who mourn, for they will be comforted" (Mathew 5:4). The condition of the world we live in should make us weep.

Fight to be dissatisfied. I agree with C.S. Lewis that one of the big problems for Christians is not that we are dissatisfied, but that we are far too easily satisfied. We can become so contented with the material sights, smells, sounds, and tastes of the physical world that we lose perspective. But if we are honest, if we mourn to see the broken world around us limping its way into hell, it will make us sick inside.

Be glad. You and I also must fight not to lose our joy and awe. Even as we fully acknowledge this broken world, we must lift our eyes to a greater truth. The Sovereign Creator God has become our Savior, and through him we are the beloved adopted children of God the Father. We must require ourselves to celebrate this every day, for all of this is the result of his grace. We must remind ourselves that Emmanuel is with us wherever we are, and in the middle of whatever we are facing.

Live with anticipation. We must recall again and again that this broken home is not our permanent address. By an extraordinary act of God's grace, all his blood-bought children are guaranteed to be part of a much better neighborhood.

Someday we will all live in the New Jerusalem on a street called Shalom, where brokenness will be no more.

Last week your boss gave you your walking papers, or your teenager rebelled to your face, or you were diagnosed with a disease, or a tree fell on your garage, or your best friend gossiped about something you said in confidence, or your aging body ached, or your church disappointed you again, or you pulled your back out, or your vacation proved to be more work than retreat, or you found out that your exorbitant city taxes are being misused by a politically hungry elected thief, or you learned that someone stole your identity, or you felt drawn to something you knew was wrong.

Last week you encountered the world as it really is: broken. How did you do?

Identity Amnesia

Identity amnesia
produces
identity replacement.
It has been
humanity's problem
since
a man and a woman
in a Garden
given as a gift
attempted to
reach up
for the
place
of Another.

3

Know Who You Are

Francine wasn't trying to run away. That's not something seventy-seven-year-old women do. She was just wandering. But once beyond the pleasant surroundings, the small geographic area familiar to her, she was truly lost. It was more than not knowing where she was. Trapped in the throes of progressive dementia, Francine wasn't quite sure *who* she was. There were ways and moments in which she seemed aware and lucid. But there were also significant gaps in her memory, gaps that made her a danger to herself and necessitated the constant care of others.

The family had come to visit Francine at the facility that was now her home. Walking the grounds with her, momentarily distracted by a lively conversation, they looked around and she was gone. A frantic yet familiar search ensued. And three minutes after fanning out in admirable imitation of a professional search-and-rescue team, her family welcomed her back into their arms with great joy and relief. Everyone hoped she would wander no more, but they all expected her to. Poor Francine did not know she was Francine anymore.

Forgetting who you are is a sad, tragic thing, an incapacitating condition. But in reality many of us are like Francine. Our dementia is not biochemical in nature, but primarily spiritual. For the Christian this is an *identity amnesia* more profound than anything poor Francine dealt with. It makes us drift and wander. We get lost and we don't know what to do about it.

Becky displayed all the symptoms of a certain variety of identity amnesia. Her approach to life might best be characterized as *spontaneous emotional reactivity*. Although Becky was a believer she did not live out of an overarching biblical identity. No, Becky tended to get her sense of internal meaning and purpose from whatever or whoever was around her at the moment. Because of this, her habit was to watch all too vigilantly. She was much too focused on how people around her interacted with and responded to her. So, in every relationship and situation, Becky rode the emotional roller coaster. She could be soaring toward joy one moment and in the next moment find herself plummeting toward despair. It was hard for her to deal with what she called "the negative stuff," and when she did she had an uncanny ability to trouble her own trouble in a way that tended to make that trouble worse.

There was no getting around it, Becky was a spiritual Francine. She simply did not know who she was, so she tended to look for identity in all the wrong places. Rather than growing in faith and courage, Becky became more paranoid and discouraged. She knew her life lacked stability but she blamed the people and circumstances around her, rather than looking within herself. Her life was an exhausting ride of radical ups and downs. Poor Becky was an identity amnesiac and didn't even know it.

If you are going to live the productive life that God's grace can enable you to live, you need to stay very clear about who you are. As I have said in previous writing, we are always living out of some sense of identity. You are constantly telling yourself who you are, and the identity you assign to yourself has much to do with how you respond to the difficulties of life. In this chapter I want to examine the two identities of every Christian. These identities are "sinner" and "child of grace." To recognize their existence and understand what it means to possess them both, together, is to see yourself as you truly are. This will profoundly shape your fundamental sense of self and radically influence for the better how you live in the here and now, somewhere between the Fall and Destiny.

Your Identity as a Sinner: Not As Good As You Thought

We all tend to be quite adept at ignoring our own sin while being highly sensitized to the sin of others. It is hard for us to receive the loving criticism, confrontation, and rebuke of others because we tend to think of ourselves as more sanctified than we actually are. As the Bible invites us to look intently into it, as into a mirror, it invites a humbling and accurate self-assessment. The biblical doctrine of sin confronts each of us with the reality that we are not as good as we imagine we are, and therefore more needy and vulnerable than we typically consider ourselves to be.

Now what does this have to do with living productively in a fallen world? It is square one. If you minimize in any way the significance of the war that goes on inside of every sinner, you will tend to minimize your own vulnerability to the daily temptations that greet us all amidst the brokenness of this world. When you underestimate your potential for temptation, you don't go through your day alert to it, planning to avoid it as you should. In that condition, temptation can easily slip past your lowered defenses, so you find yourself tricked and deceived again and again. There's no mystery here. You were unprepared because you did not enter the situation with a humble sense of your own sinfulness.

It is also true that when you minimize the presence and power of the sin that remains in you, you do not reach out for the help of God and others. Self-righteousness can cause us to try to live more independently than God ever intended. We do not reach out for help because, frankly, we do not think we need it. So we live independent and self-sufficient lives, the kind we were never hardwired to live. Trying to live independent of the daily intervention of God and others is like trying to bake a cake in a washing machine. That washing machine is a wonderful creation, but it was never designed to do what you are asking it to do. All you will end up with is a soapy batter, a dirty machine, and a badly dented pan!

Productive living is always rooted in a humble sense of personal neediness. This neediness only comes when you begin to understand and accept what the Bible has to say about sin, and daily reach out for the help that can only be found through the Lord Jesus Christ.

The Sad News About Sin

On the off chance that you haven't noticed already—or, more likely, that you haven't considered it recently—here's something you must bear in mind. There will be a war in your heart between what the Bible has to say about you and what you would like to think is true about you. You and I tend to think we are wiser and more sanctified than we actually are. That is why we get defensive when someone points out our sin and weakness. I become defensive when what people say about me doesn't agree with my view of myself. It feels like I am being misjudged.

This is why I need to remember constantly that the Bible is the world's best diagnostic tool. When I look into the mirror of the Word of God, I see the exact essence of who I am. Only when I am willing to embrace the sadness of seeing myself accurately can I experience the joyful grace that God gives to those who acknowledge their need.

This means that, although I am constantly tempted to think otherwise, I must face the fact that my greatest need is not *environmental*. My greatest need does not derive from the fact that the brokenness of the Fall fractures every situation, every relationship, and every context. Yes, all my relationships are flawed in some way. And no, the world around me does not operate as God intended. But this environmental brokenness is not my greatest, deepest, most abiding problem. No matter what I face in this fallen world, my greatest problem in life exists inside of me and not outside of me. Sure, I want to think that it is . . .

My spouse
My children
My neighbors
My extended family
My history
My church
My job
My friends
My boss
My community
My finances
The government
The traffic
The Internet
Society in general
And the list could go on and on.

But the Bible tells me something very different. Even though my environment has been broken by sin, my biggest problem is *moral*. There is something wrong inside of *me*, and in one way or another it influences everything I desire, think, choose, say, and do. Scripture uses three words to flesh out this truth.

They can be found in Psalm 51, one of the Bible's best descriptions of our internal moral problem.

"Have mercy on me, O God, according to your unfailing love; according to your great compassion blot out my *transgressions*. Wash away all my *iniquity* and cleanse me from my *sin*" (Psalm 51:1–2). Here David gives us three words that capture and define who we are and how great our need actually is: transgression, iniquity, and sin. Let's examine each separately.

Transgression of the Rebellious

To transgress is to know where the boundaries are and willingly step over them. I transgress when I park in a spot clearly marked "No Parking." I know I am not supposed to park there, but at the moment I don't care what the law says. I am focused only on comfort and convenience. I don't want to look for another space, especially if it means walking further to my destination after leaving the car. Ruled by selfish desires, I willingly park where parking is prohibited.

Something similar happens in many other areas of life. We know God has forbidden what we are about to do, but just now we do not care. For the moment, God's will and the call of his kingdom and glory are not in our eyes, or ruling our hearts. In that moment our hearts are ruled by a desire for our own satisfaction, comfort, power, pleasure, independence, or success. So we pursue what we want and step over the boundaries we know God has set for us. Perhaps this means being nasty in order to win an argument. Or maybe it means working longer hours than is spiritually healthy for my family. Or it could mean cheating on an exam. Or it may involve low-balling my income to save on my taxes. Or it could mean eating too much or indulging in thoughts I should immediately reject.

Yet transgression goes even deeper than this. I am not merely willing to deny God's authority by transgressing his boundaries. In an effort to suppress my conscience and explain away my guilt, I also try to convince myself, in effect, that I am a better king than God is. I preach to myself the false gospel that my moral system is superior to and more efficient than the one God gave me. I tell myself that I am better off ruling myself than following God. So, motivated by the moral laws of personal wants, needs, and feelings, I step over God's boundaries, fully aware of the wrong I am doing but committed to doing it anyway.

Transgression is high-handed and rebellious. Transgression is about arrogant moments of self-rule. Transgression is about shocking pride that is able to convince me that I know better than God does. Transgression is bold-faced, autonomous, I-am-my-own-authority living.

All of us transgress God's boundaries again and again. But not every act of sin is high-handed rebellion against God's wise authority. So David employs a second word: *iniquity*.

Iniquity of the Soiled

Where *transgression* speaks of a particular variety of sin and its motivations, *iniquity* emphasizes the result of sin working within each of us. Iniquity is moral uncleanness, produced by indwelling sin. Sin within us is a moral infection that corrupts everything we desire, think, say, and do. This infection reaches to every aspect of my being. There is nothing in me that remains untainted.

It is stunning to consider, but not a single aspect of my being is morally pure. Every infant except the Lord has come into the world with an untreatable condition, the pervasive infection of iniquity. Yet I desperately want to see myself as an exception, to hold on to some faint hope of independent moral purity. Talk about self-delusion! I want to imagine I am clean in myself, like Christ! But I am not, and there is nothing I can do to change that. The presence of iniquity is total (it includes all of us) and comprehensive (it reaches to every aspect of our personhood). Nevertheless, we cling to a fantasy of our own purity, even as we hypocritically point out the moral infection in those around us.

Sin of the Weak

There is a third word David uses to describe our moral problem: *sin*. If iniquity is moral uncleanness, then sin is moral weakness. Sin has left me weak, foolish, and incapable of consistently obeying God. Even if I were to desire always to do what is right, I don't have the power to follow through. In my sin, I consistently fall short of God's standards. Sin renders me unable to keep God's law. I find myself falling short over and over again. I fall short in my conversations. I fall short in my marriage and in my parenting. I fall short in times of work and leisure. I fall short in my desires and my thoughts. There is not a day that goes by that I do not fall short in some way.

The Root of All Lies: "You Don't Have Enough"

Transgression, *iniquity*, and *sin* are three words that unpack the moral dilemma that is the most important drama of the Christian's life. But no child of God can get by recognizing only his or her identity as sinner. The weight of it will defeat you, and to press you toward defeat the enemy will spin out endless variations of the lie that he first told in the Garden and has been repeating ever since. This lie is meant to discourage and divert you. It is meant to force you into moral timidity and ethical paralysis. Everyone who has been given the humility to see himself with accuracy, everyone who has come to admit that he might, in fact, be something less than righteous in himself, is susceptible to this lie. This lie even grows in plausibility when you examine your track record or assess this fallen world honestly. The essence of this horrible, deceptive, and ultimately blasphemous lie can be expressed in just four words, words that have the power to alter how you live. Here they are: "You don't have enough."

The lie comes in a thousand forms. "You don't have enough to deal with the struggles of thought and desire that war inside you every day." "You don't have enough to deal with that neighbor who seems more committed to his rose garden than he is to having a cordial relationship with you." "You don't have enough to live in a God-honoring relationship of love, unity, and understanding with your spouse." "You don't have enough to parent those children God has given you, who you wish would be compliant just once!" "You don't have enough to deal with that boss who never seems able to be satisfied and thankful." "You don't have enough to love the people around you who are rude and critical, or different from you." "You don't have enough to fight the idolatry of materialism that greets you every day in Western culture." "You simply don't have enough!"

When you allow the poison of this lie to begin to seep into the cells of your heart, you will quit living with faith, hope, and courage. You will quit living with expectancy. You will quit looking for the good things God will do outside of you, inside of you, and through you. You will begin to live cautiously and self-protectively. And you will end up giving way to things that, by God's grace, you actually have the power to fight. You will end up settling for a human, second-best, survivalist lifestyle, a lifestyle several rungs lower than the life of faith and hope to which God has called you.

So yes, you are a sinner. And if that were all, the enemy would be right: you certainly would not have enough. But you are more than a sinner. You are also a child of grace.

Your Identity as a Child of Grace: Better Than You Can Imagine

To become a Christian is to be given a new nature, a new identity. You don't lose the old identity (yet), but you do receive a down payment on who you will be. Therefore, while it is vital to accept your identity as a sinner, it is *not* sufficient. You must also live out of a sure grasp of your identity as a child of God's freely given and personally transforming grace. These two identities must be held in a healthy tension and balance. It is only the person who is deeply aware of his sin who gets excited about grace, and it is only grace that can give you the courage to humbly face the enormity of your sin.

Grace is the most transformational word in Scripture. The entire Bible is a narrative of God's grace, a story of undeserved redemption. By the transformational power of his grace, God unilaterally reaches into the muck of this fallen world, through the presence of his Son, and radically transforms his children from what we are (sinners) into what we are becoming by his power (Christ-like). The famous Newton hymn uses the best word possible for that grace, *amazing*.

So grace is a story and grace is a gift. It is God's character and it is your hope. Grace is a transforming tool and a state of relationship. Grace is a theology and an invitation. Grace is an experience and a calling. Grace will turn your life upside down while giving you a rest you have never known. Grace will convince you of your unworthiness without ever making you feel unloved.

Grace will make you acknowledge that you cannot earn God's favor, and it will remove your fear of not measuring up to his standards. Grace will confront you with the fact that you are much less than you thought you were, even as it assures you that you can be far more than you had ever imagined. Grace will put you in your place without ever putting you down.

Grace will enable you to face truths about yourself that you have hesitated to consider, while freeing you from being self-consciously introspective. Grace will confront you with profound weaknesses, and at the same time introduce you to new-found strength. Grace will tell you what you aren't, while welcoming you to what you can now be. Grace will make you as uncomfortable as you have ever been, while offering you more comfort than you have ever known. Grace will drive you to the end of yourself, while it invites you to fresh starts and new beginnings. Grace will dash your hopes, but never leave you hopeless. Grace will decimate your kingdom as it introduces you to a better King. Grace will expose your blindness as it gives you eyes to see. Grace will make you sadder than you have ever been, while it gives you greater cause for celebration than you have ever known.

Grace enters your life in a moment and will occupy you for eternity. You simply cannot live a productive life in this broken-down world unless you have a practical grasp of the grace you have been given.

The Good News about Grace

Grace enters your life in three powerful forms. These aspects of God's grace really do have the power to undo you and rebuild you once again.

The Grace of Forgiveness

Perhaps it will take an eternity for us to understand the extent of the grace we have been given, and the significance of the forgiveness that flows from that grace. But this much is certain, no other force in this life compares to forgiveness in its power to change the way you live. There is a wonderful moment in the life of Christ that powerfully exhibits this. Jesus is having dinner at the house of a Pharisee.

Now one of the Pharisees invited Jesus to have dinner with him, so he went to the Pharisee's house and reclined at the table. When a woman who had lived a sinful life in that town learned that Jesus was eating at the Pharisee's house, she brought an alabaster jar of perfume, and as she stood behind him at his feet weeping, she began to wet his feet with her tears. Then she wiped them with her hair, kissed them and poured perfume on them.

When the Pharisee who had invited him saw this, he said to himself, "If this man were a prophet, he would know who is touching him and what kind of woman she is—that she is a sinner."

Jesus answered him, "Simon, I have something to tell you."

"Tell me, teacher," he said.

"Two men owed money to a certain moneylender. One owed him five hundred denarii, and the other fifty. Neither of them had the money to pay him back, so he canceled the debts of both. Now which of them will love him more?"

Simon replied, "I suppose the one who had the bigger debt canceled."

"You have judged correctly," Jesus said.

Then he turned toward the woman and said to Simon, "Do you see this woman? I came into your house. You did not give me any water for my feet, but she wet my feet with her tears and wiped them with her hair. You did not give me a kiss, but this woman, from the time I entered, has not stopped kissing my feet. You did not put oil on my head, but she has poured perfume on my feet. Therefore, I tell you, her many sins have been forgiven—for she loved much. But he who has been forgiven little loves little."

—Luke 7:36–47

Why did this woman do this expensive and humbling thing? Why the ointment of her tears? Why her many kisses? There is only one plausible answer, the answer set forth in the passage: forgiveness. When you grasp how much you need it, and when, by God's grace, you reach out and receive it, it changes you forever.

Forgiveness is the goal of God's redemptive story. It is the plan that God began implementing from the moment Adam and Eve disobeyed. In doing this, God used his creative power to harness the elements of nature. He used his sovereign authority to order the events of human history. He controlled it all so that at the perfect moment the Lord Jesus Christ would come to earth, be born in a town in Palestine, face with perfect sinlessness the realities of life in a broken and sinful world, be betrayed by one of his followers, be convicted by a corrupt court, be sentenced to death by a self-interested politician, die a criminal's death, but as the perfect Lamb of God exit his borrowed tomb as victor over both sin and death.

Why did he do all this? Because you and I were born as sinners and our sin has left us guilty before God. Forgiveness, Christ's gift to us, means that we can stand before God in all of our neediness, weakness, and moral failure and yet be utterly unafraid. Sinful people can stand before a Holy God because Jesus took the penalty for our sin on himself and satisfied the Father's anger. Sin leaves me guilty, but forgiveness relieves my guilt.

It is amazing to think that all my sins of the past, all my sins of the present, and all my sins of the future have been fully and completely covered by the blood of the Lord Jesus Christ. I do not have to work to excuse what I have done. I do not have to mollify my conscience with rationalizations. I do not have to ease my guilt with arguments for my own righteousness. I do not have to try to make myself feel better about what I have done by blaming someone else. No, I can stand before God just as I am, without fear, because in Jesus Christ I am fully and completely forgiven. Anytime I work to erect some system of self-justification I have committed an act of gospel irrationality. It makes no sense to try to justify my sin, because each sinful act—past, present, and future—has already been forgiven by the grace of God.

But forgiveness doesn't just call you out of the hiding of self-righteousness and self-justification. It mobilizes you. The minute you begin to grasp the magnitude of the forgiveness you have been given, you want others to experience it. You want the people around you to know the personal rest and hope that only forgiveness provides. What really brings you joy is the people around you coming to know the One who has offered you such amazing forgiveness. And forgiveness does something else, too. It makes you want to obey. Forgiveness draws your heart in love and thankfulness to God, and in your love for him you desire to think, do, and say things that are pleasing to him.

The Grace of Enablement

Once confidence in God's forgiveness has called you out of hiding to confess that you have lived the wrong way, something new will greet you: the fear that you don't have what it takes to live as you should. Your fear will be well-founded. Sin not only leave us guilty, it leaves us unable. It cripples our ability to be what we are supposed to be and do what we are supposed to do. This is why we need the grace of enablement. Along with forgiveness, we need power.

That power does not come through some impersonal force. It does not come as enhanced personal strength. The power that God gives me is not a thing. God gives me a Person. To provide for me the strength I need to live in the way he has designed, God gives me the only thing that can truly help me. He gives me himself. The Spirit of God unzips me and gets inside me, enabling me to desire, think, do, and say the things that fit within the boundaries of his plan and purpose for me (See Galatians 2:20 and Ephesians 3:20). This is how every Christian can live with the moment-by-moment assurance that God will never assign a task without giving the grace to accomplish it. He animates and strengthens me with his presence, so that I can say "no" to sin and "yes" to the call of his kingdom.

The Grace of Deliverance

There is one final thing you need to know in order to understand the grace that has been bestowed on you: you are loved by a dissatisfied Redeemer. He will not rest from his work of grace until every last microbe of sin has been completely

46

eradicated from every last cell of every last one of his children. And so he wars against sin on our behalf. We are never alone in our struggle for a single moment. We never have to deal with the temptations of a situation or relationship by ourselves. He is absolutely resolute in his determination that every one of his children will experience the complete spoils of the victory he gained over sin and death through his crucifixion and resurrection.

You are blessed every day by his dissatisfaction. You are blessed every day that he does not grow discouraged, tired, or weary. You are blessed every day that he rules over all things for your sake. You are blessed every day that to cease from any of this he would have to deny himself, and that is something he will never do.

There will be a day when you are invited to the one funeral you will actually want to attend. This funeral won't bring grief to your heart or tears to your eyes. This funeral will make you sing and celebrate. This funeral will make you wonder how you could have been chosen to be the recipient of such blessing. There will be a day when you will attend the funeral of sin. Sin will die and you will live forever, permanently freed from the tyranny of sin.

These two identities, *sinner* and *child of grace*, are the pillars that support a restoration lifestyle and a healthy and productive life on this side of eternity. My identity as a sinner daily confronts me with how deep and pervasive my need actually is. My identity as a child of grace confronts me with how expansive my potential actually is. It is only when I humbly admit my identity as a sinner that I live as a consumer of the grace of God, and it is only when I am comforted by my identity as a child of grace that I will be able to look honestly at the magnitude of my sin.

Sinner and child of grace; there is simply no replacement for an accurate knowledge of who you really are.

Secret Wish

Perhaps
it's the secret wish
of every soul
struggling in the middle
of what he did not plan
and did not choose.
Perhaps
it is the silent cry
of each of us
as we are forced to deal
with someone
who is difficult to love.
Perhaps
we all think that
we're wiser than we really are
and more benevolent
than we would actually be.
Perhaps
we all forget that
sin has reduced us to fools
and shrunk our field of interest
to the size of our own needs.
Perhaps
that's why all of us
secretly wish to be
sovereign.

4

Rest in God's Sovereignty

I did it again and again when our children resisted our instruction and correction. I did it again and again when they debated a command or questioned our plans. I did it again and again when they opposed our authority and quested for self-rule. I did it again and again for two good reasons.

To begin with, my wife and I had brought children into this world who thought they didn't need us! Each of them at some point fell into believing they were far more knowledgeable and capable than they really were. They all assumed that their intentions were noble and their plans were sound. They all thought they were capable of determining what was best, even when they lacked important information and experience. They simply felt they were in possession of a better way.

But there was a second reason I did it again and again. Our children were too young to grasp the abstract, strategic, and often theological purposes underlying my instruction. Even if I explained everything in as age-appropriate a way as I could, they would still have no actual understanding. They just did not yet have the categories or the capacity to grasp the parental logic behind the plan or command.

So I did the same thing again and again. I would kneel down in front of them at eye level and say, "Please look at Daddy's face. Do you know how much I love you? Do you know that your Daddy is not a mean, bad man? Do you know that I would never ask you to do anything that would hurt you or make you sick? I am sorry that you can't understand why Daddy is asking you to do this. I wish I could explain it to you, but you are too young to understand. So I am going to ask you to do something—trust Daddy. When you walk down the hallway to do what Daddy has asked you to do, say to yourself, 'My Daddy loves me. My Daddy would never ask me to do something bad. I am going to trust my Daddy and stop trying to be the Daddy of my Daddy.'"

God does the same thing with you, over and over again. He meets you in one of the difficult hallways of your life, kneels down before you in condescending love, and asks you to trust his loving and wise rule, even though you don't have a clue what he is doing. He knows there are many times when your life doesn't look like there is anyone ruling it, let alone someone wise and good. He knows there will be times when you will wish you could write your own story. He knows that at times you will be overwhelmed by what is on your plate. He knows that his plan will confuse and confound you. And he knows that real rest cannot be found in understanding. Real rest is found in trust. So he is willing to have the conversation with you again and again, and he has made sure that his Word assures you of his rule again and again. (For just a few examples, see 1 Chronicles 29:11–12, Psalm 103:19, Psalm 115:3, Proverbs 21:1, Isaiah 46:9–10, Daniel 4:35, and Ephesians 1:11.)

Our Sovereign Fantasy

Like children, we all buy into a fundamental and very tempting delusion. Our weakness in this area is what gave an opening to the serpent in the Garden, and by it that same enemy still seeks to prey upon us today. There are two helpful ways of expressing and thinking about this delusion, although in practice these two forms are so closely related as to produce what is essentially a single fantasy.

The first and primary form of this delusion is *autonomy*. To be truly autonomous is to be independent, self-determining, and self-ruling. To possess autonomy is to have the right to do with your time and resources whatever you will. It means you can set your own rules and chart your own course, that you are in charge of your own life and nobody has the authority to tell you what to do.

It doesn't take much reflection to see how irrational and even absurd this notion is. Imagine if all the drivers in Philadelphia, where I live, began to drive as if they actually thought they were autonomous. Imagine the chaos and carnage that would ensue as the desires of one driver collided head-on with the desires of another driver, throughout the city!

Autonomy is a delusion that seduces all of us. Every time I treat my wife, children, or friends in a way I should not treat them, in order to advance my own purpose, I am operating out of the delusion of autonomy. Every time I take for myself glory that belongs to God, I am claiming autonomy. Every time I willingly step over one of God's boundaries with a word, a thought, a choice, or an action, I am acting as if my life belonged to me. Autonomy is a dangerous fantasy that at various times and in various ways deceives us all.

Another way to think about this same basic delusion is in terms of *self-sufficiency*. To be self-sufficient is to have everything you need within yourself to be what you were designed to be, and to do what you were designed to do.

To assume we are self-sufficient is no more rational than to assume we are autonomous. Obviously, a newborn child is the opposite of self-sufficient, while young children and teens clearly have their own limitations. But what about a mature, accomplished adult? What about you? Can you be self-sufficient?

Here's a test. Consider all the things you have done in the last twenty-four hours that required the assistance or contributions of others. Did you sleep indoors? Travel in a vehicle? Use electricity? Wear clothing you didn't make? Read? Eat food you didn't kill or grow? Get water from a faucet? Would any of that have been possible without the involvement of countless other people?

We were designed to live in worshipful dependence upon God and in humble, interdependent community with other people. Self-sufficiency may be a nonsensical delusion, but it is a powerfully seductive and dangerous one. Yet every day we act as if we're far more independent than we actually are. Every time you are too proud to ask for help, you buy into the fantasy of your self-sufficiency. Every time you reject someone who is trying to confront you with a wrong, you are believing the lie of your self-sufficiency. Every time you act like you know more than you actually know, you accept the delusion of your self-sufficiency.

The Confrontation of Nature

God designed this world in such a way that it serves as a constant reminder of his presence, his character, and his glory. Even as creation reminds us of these divine attributes, it does something else. It confronts our delusions of autonomy and self-sufficiency.

The doctrine of creation reveals the delusion of autonomy for the foolishness it is. Think about the logic here. If there is a Creator and you are his creature, the work of his hands, then there is no such thing as autonomy.

I am a painter by avocation. When, after months of work, I finally complete a painting, who does that painting belong to? The answer is easy and obvious. It belongs to me because I created it. Does the beauty or sophistication of the thing created change who owns it? No. If somehow my next painting were judged by every art critic in the world to be the single best painting in history, it would still be mine, and I could still do with it whatever I pleased. In the same way, we belong to God, however amazingly well-constructed we are or imagine ourselves to be.

You cannot embrace both the doctrine of creation and the illusion of personal autonomy. The first cancels out the second. The Bible begins by declaring that the entire physical world (including humans) is the product of God's creative artistry. It follows from this that we are owned by him. Therefore, he alone has the right to tell us how we should participate in the existence that is his creation.

The doctrine of creation also exposes the lie of self-sufficiency. You can plant the healthiest seeds available, but if God doesn't send the rain your plants will die. You are dependent on God for your very life and breath. If he would withdraw his hand this orderly world would explode into chaos. Look how a drought or a flood can bring a region to its knees. Look at all the examples of how the goods of one part of the world are desperately needed by another part of the world. The more you consider the interdependent operation of the various elements of creation, the clearer it is that no aspect of God's creation is truly self-sufficient, including you.

Especially you.

The Struggle

With all this being true, and even obvious, it is remarkable that we still struggle to accept and rest in God's sovereignty! We all hit those moments when we think we know better. We all fall into thinking we have a better plan. We all try to pick through the mysteries of our own existence, trying to figure out things we simply don't have the capacity to understand. And we all act at one time or another as if we were the fourth member of the Trinity, seeking to control things beyond our grasp and making the mess that we struggle with even messier. It is worthwhile, therefore, to examine our struggle with God's sovereignty and our lack of sovereignty.

Here are some things that each of us will grapple with as we live in this broken-down house. Each one involves the issue of control. Each one emerges from our delusions of autonomy and self-sufficiency. And each one is resolved when we yield our hearts and minds to God's sovereign, loving care.

You Will Be Confronted with Your Lack of Control

June was banking on her plan. The firm she had longed to work with for years had guaranteed her a dream job, so she let go of her apartment and gave notice at the office. Her life was boxed up and ready to go. She had said her goodbyes to friends and family and now was just waiting for Saturday, when the moving truck would arrive. But on Tuesday the bottom fell out of her future company and its stock value collapsed. It was the financial news of the week. By Friday, the firm was no more.

John woke up weary. He would spend another day as a caregiver for his profoundly handicapped wife. He loved her and was not bitter against her in any way. He was just tired. It wasn't supposed to be this way. They had had their life all planned out, until her accident changed everything. The lawsuit had taken care of them financially, but John seemed unable to stop asking why his wife had been so horribly injured.

Cheryl was very aware that she had been blessed by growing up in a godly and loving family. There had never been a genuine need in her life that wasn't taken care of. In her heart she knew that her very existence had been shaped by God.

Whether it's due to a single life-altering event, or a thousand small daily reminders, you can't go very long without somehow, some way being confronted with your lack of control. Of course, you're not alone in this. We all have the exact same problem. Except God.

You Will Wish You Had More Power

Is there any area of life where we do not sometimes wish we had more power and ability? A vital part of our calling as God's creatures and image-bearers is to be good stewards in those areas where God has granted us responsibility. Yet no matter how much responsibility or authority we have been given, and no matter how diligently we seek to develop our gifts and talents, there is not a single area of life in which our power is absolute. There is always a ceiling beyond which we cannot go, an area completely outside our grasp, no matter how much we might crave or strive for it. But that doesn't keep us from wishing for more power, does it?

A mom who was struggling with the scary rebellion and unbelief of her two teenage boys epitomized this desire when she said, "If it's the last thing I ever do, I will get my boys to believe!" For the sake of her sons, this mom craved a power no one can possess. She wanted to plant saving faith directly into their hearts, and that is not an ability God has granted us.

Parenting, of course, is just one possible example among many. It is so easy to believe that if you simply had more power in a particular area, your life would immediately be better. The fact is that if God had granted us more power, in our sinfulness we would be very skilled at troubling our own trouble. It is the grace of God that limits our power and ability because there is nothing we can wield—no tool, no power, no ability, no authority, no privilege—that we are not inclined to distort and abuse.

You Will Be Tempted to Think Your World Is out of Control

Another mark of our delusional self-centeredness is that, when we encounter an area that we cannot control, we tend to see it as *out* of control! We need to understand that God's sense of order is very different from ours. What looks like utter confusion to us is actually a discrete piece of divine planning, every time. But in the finiteness of our understanding, wisdom, and experience, it is often hard to see the order.

Here is the struggle: Just as you cannot be a good steward without seeking to exercise a measure of control, you cannot be a responsible human being without planning. You and I have been given the capacity to peer into the future, to envision a desirable outcome, and to conceive a set of steps that will get us there. Once we have settled on a plan and committed to it, we want our plan to unfold as intended. So it is usually hard to see interruptions and obstacles as good or orderly. In fact they often tempt us to doubt God's sovereignty, or his goodness, or both.

Now add to this the fact that the world in which we live is a broken-down house that is not functioning as designed. The result is that our expectations become confused and our desires confounded, making everything more difficult. So in each of our lives there are moments when we feel like screaming, "Is anyone in charge here?" Actually, yes. God is.

You Will Fear the Power of Another

When you question or lose sight of the good and perfect rule of the Lord, you can end up fearing the power of another. Whether a malevolent hidden terrorist, a very real and immoral relative, or a pure figment of your imagination, you will perceive someone as having character and intentions that tempt you to anxiety.

Maybe your boss is unethical and you fear being caught in the web of his deceit. Maybe your dad is increasingly angry and you fear that his anger will explode in your direction. Maybe your wife is at her wits' end and you fear she may lose it with the children when you are out of the house. Maybe someone from your past is holding on to a misunderstanding and you are concerned it may ultimately harm your reputation. Or maybe you just struggle with all the nameless people in places unknown whose dark decisions may affect your life in some way: politicians, corporations, Wall Street, the news media, Hollywood, etc.

Only when you are comforted by the fact of God's ultimate, comprehensive, flawless, holy authority, can you stop being afraid of human authority. When you truly know that the "king's heart is in the hand of the LORD" (Proverbs 21:1), you can be freed from the anxiety of flawed human rule.

You Will Be Tempted to Question God's Wisdom and Love

God's sovereignty will inevitably take you where you did not intend to go. He will bless you with things you could not possibly have earned or achieved. But God will also choose for you to go through things that are difficult, and to endure things that are painful. In those moments—some of which may stretch into quite lengthy seasons—you will be tempted to question his wisdom, or his love, or both.

It is so easy to conjure up in your imagination how much better your life would be had you been able to direct it yourself, deciding what you were going to face and when. "Why couldn't God have done things more like I would have? Why did he have to choose this path?" It is tempting to let the thought seep into your heart that if God really loved you, he wouldn't have allowed into your life some particular challenge or area of difficulty.

To question the love of him who died for us is a testimony to our own frailty. To question the wisdom of the One in whom all things hold together (Colossians 1:17) is a testimony to our own foolishness. The ease with which we question our loving Father ought not to be a matter of condemnation for us, but it should promote our humility.

You Will Think That Rest Requires Understanding

It is not a sin to desire to understand. Your rationality is a gift of your Creator. Your ability to reason, analyze, interpret, organize, and explain is one of the things that sets you apart from the rest of creation. You should endeavor to know everything you can about God, his character, and his plan for the world and the people he has placed in it. Yet you cannot allow the analytical power of your mind to be the source of your hope, confidence, and continuance. You will not always understand; in truth, there are few if any things about this infinitely complex creation that we finite creatures truly understand.

You and I are exactly like the illustration of my children I used in the beginning of this chapter. We think we would find it much easier to obey if we grasped all the details about why we are being asked to do one thing or another. But this desire to understand is simply another form of the desire to control. We want to have the option of signing off on God's plan, just in case there's something he overlooked. Yet at the same time we know we don't have the capacity to understand God's creation fully.

We simply need to accept that the reasons God does what he does in our lives, or how our life fits into the whole of his grand redemptive plan, will never be completely clear in this life. This is why real rest and peace is not found in knowing and understanding. It is only found in trust. Only when you have a quiet confidence in the Lord behind the plan and have come to know his love, wisdom, power, and grace, will you be able to rest in hope—even when you do not understand what God is doing in a particular moment in your life. This is exactly the experience expressed in Psalm 33:20–21, "We wait in hope for the LORD; he is our help and our shield. In him our hearts rejoice, for we trust in his holy name."

Someone Else's Life Will Look Better Than Yours

It is very easy to look around and begin to wonder why God has singled us out for what feels like unusual difficulty, when the life of the person next to us seems to be blessed with ease. There are even times when we reason (in rather shocking self-righteousness) that we are more deserving (because we are obviously more holy) than the guy next to us who seems to have it so easy. In moments like this you begin to wonder if it is really worth it to obey. This is the exact struggle that is unfolded, and resolved, in Psalm 73.

You Will Reach a Place of Greater Rest in God's Rule

After all this—your fear and confusion, your struggles with control, and your "need" to understand—you will come to a new place of faith. In fact, as God continues to mature you to make you more like his Son, you'll undoubtedly run through this entire cycle over and over again! But through it all, at no point will God leave you alone to flounder your way through. He is a God of magnificent grace and patient love.

Listen to what Jesus said to his disciples as he was preparing to leave them. "I have much more to say to you, more than you can now bear. But when he, the Spirit of truth, comes, he will guide you into all truth. He will not speak on his own; he will speak only what he hears, and he will tell you what is yet to come" (John 16:12–13). Your Lord is not only the *source* of your rest. He loves you so much that he works to bring you to a greater level of real-life, practical confidence in his wise rule and therefore to a greater and more frequent personal *experience* of rest, even in the face of mystery and difficulty. The longer you follow him, and the more you tire of the fruit of your own anxiety, the more you are willing to walk down another hallway of your life and say, "I don't know exactly what my Father is doing, but I do know that my Father loves me, and I do know that he is good."

A Picture of Sovereign Care

So, what does God's sovereign care actually look like? There is probably no better summary description than the one Paul gives us at the end of the first chapter of Ephesians. There, Paul speaks of God's "incomparably great power for us who believe." He goes on,

That power is like the working of his mighty strength, which he exerted in Christ when he raised him from the dead and seated him at his right hand in the heavenly realms, far above all rule and authority, power and dominion, and every title that can be given, not only in the present age but also in the one to come. And God placed all things under his feet and appointed him to be head over everything for the church, which is his body, the fullness of him who fills everything in every way.

—Ephesians 1:19–23

There are three truths to be seen here about the sovereign rule of King Christ, the rule that is meant to be your most reliable source of rest as you live in that space between the difficulties of life in this broken world and the mysteries of God's plan. As Paul tells us, that rule is *comprehensive*, *personal*, and *redemptive*.

First, Paul wants you to know that the rule of your Redeemer is *comprehensive*. Paul says that God placed "all things under his feet" and appointed him "head over everything." You could not choose language that would be more all-inclusive than this. What this tells us, in the clearest possible terms, is that you will never find yourself in a location, situation, or relationship that is not ruled by King Christ.

Second, Paul wants you to know that the rule of your Lord is *personal*. Paul says that he rules over everything "for the church, which is his body." His rule is exercised for your sake. You are not a pawn in some great chess match. You are not an expendable player in anybody's game. You are the child of a Father whose Son had to die so you could be adopted. Your Father rules in sovereign love. His eye is on you and his ear is open to your cry. He cares about you, permanently and deeply. And in ways you often will not be able to understand in the moment, he controls all things for your benefit. (See also Acts 17:26–28.)

Finally, Paul wants us to know that God's rule is *redemptive*. The whole context of these verses is the transforming grace that is the central attribute and gift of God's rule. His rule really is a rule of grace. His promises to us are trustworthy and reliable because of his rulership. He can guarantee us his grace because he controls all the situations, relationships, and locations where that grace will do its transforming work.

In this broken world you need a place to run for comfort, encouragement, motivation, strength, and rest. There is no better place to run than into the arms of the One who reigns over it all for your sake. No, you won't always understand. Yes, there will be moments when life will seem overwhelmingly difficult. Sure, you will wonder why he has chosen you to go through what you are enduring when the person next to you seems to have it so easy. And there will be times when you are tempted to question his wisdom and love. But in those moments, determine to do this one thing. Determine to run to him and not from him. Run to him with your questions, doubts, confusion, and fear. He loves you; he will not turn you away. He wants you to know rest. This is precisely what he has told you again and again in his Word—that he is in control, so that in those moments when you are confronted with your lack of control, or when life seems out of control, you would know peace. Not because you understand what is happening, but because you know and trust your Father.

Isn't it wonderful to know that no matter how difficult and confusing life may be, no matter how unexpected and alarming your circumstances may be, there is rest to be found? This rest is found, not in knowing the future or in logical syllogisms, and not in research or experience. No, rest is a gift of grace. It is the result of being accepted into the family of the King of Kings and Lord of lords. Rest is found in knowing that the One who rules it all is your Father. Rest is knowing that the King loves you with an everlasting love and he rules over all things for your sake. This kind of rest will stay with you when circumstances are wonderful and when they are terrible, because your rest isn't circumstantial, it is personal. Now that's real rest!

Awake Again

Awake again,
knowledge of another day
like the previous,
authored
by the pen of Another.
My own narrative
unknown to me
before
the chapters unfold.
Things to be faced
unknown to me
before
I face them.
Dreams come
of prophetic vision
more power
greater control.
In a world broken
with people flawed,
in the middle
of daily mystery
where questions multiply
and answers flee,
it is a constant battle
to accept
your limits.

5

Admit Your Limits

*R*ianna's anger, frustration, and discouragement grew each day. There were things about Sol that drove her crazy, and she watched him with the hyper-vigilance of a prison guard. His behavior could embarrass her in public, and in private bring her personal pain. *He has good qualities, he really does,* she would tell herself, but it never quieted her anger or diminished her resolve to change him. He seemed to have an uncanny ability to push her buttons, and there were days when she was irritated with him before breakfast even began. Sure, many of the things that bothered her about him had been obvious before they were married, but now the constant exposure was far worse than she had anticipated. She had always thought of herself as patient, but her patience was nearly gone.

It all came to a head one evening at dinner. Sol was doing what he usually did at meals. Hunched over his plate, he was attending to his food with all the subtlety of a commercial-grade shop vac, yet somehow he also seemed critical and unappreciative. In a fit of pent-up anger and frustration, Rianna stood up and grabbed his plate. Sol reached out to take it back and the plate went crashing to the floor. Rianna yelled, "I told myself that once we were married I could change you, but it's just hopeless!" and stormed upstairs to the bedroom.

As she lay there crying, her words kept echoing in her brain, *I told myself I could change you . . . I told myself I could change you . . .* And in a flash of insight, Rianna began to understand something very important, something it would take months for her to fully grasp and admit. She wasn't angry simply because Sol had some obvious areas of immaturity. Mostly she was angry at the faulty commitment she had made to herself as she was entering the marriage. Rianna was frustrated because she had vowed that she would change her husband—a failed mission from day one. The only result was that Sol felt incessantly watched and criticized, and Rianna felt like a personal and marital failure.

Rianna was about to do the hardest thing she had done in her adult life. She was about to admit and accept her limits in this area. Too long had she lived with messianic intentions. Too long had she overestimated her power. Too long had she pursued a task only God could accomplish. It was going to be hard to let go. It was going to be a challenge to entrust Sol into God's hands, but she was ready to try and knew she must.

Delusions of Grandeur

Rianna is not alone. When it comes to our relationships, many of us have taken on a job only God can accomplish. As we get to know people and experience their flaws firsthand, it can be very tempting to try to change them in some way. In doing this, we presume to rise to the throne of the Creator, that we might remake someone in our own image. So the intellectual, analytical wife determines she is going to clone her machine-like husband into her image because she simply can't stand the fact that he doesn't have any desire to read the great books she has read. Or the dad, fearing that his son won't exercise personal faith in Christ, takes on the role of savior and attempts to force his son to believe. His hyper-vigilant criticism of the son's lack of faith just pushes the boy further away. Or as you get to know a friend, there is a particular habit you think is rude or immature and, maybe without even being conscious of it, you make it your job to change that person in that area.

In fact, you and I change no one. Ultimately, personal change comes from only one source: the gracious act of a powerful God. When people try to change one another, typically the focus is on behavior. Yet behavior is not really the issue. If a person's words, actions, choices, decisions, reactions, or responses are other than what God would want them to be, then the root problem is not behavior, but the heart.

The heart is the core of our personhood, and the source of behavioral causality. What a person says or does is shaped by the thoughts and desires of the heart (see Luke 6:43–45). Heart change is always the result of the grace of God. You and I simply have no ability whatsoever to change the heart of another human being. We are never anything more than tools of change in the hands of a powerful, wise, and loving Redeemer. When we attempt to do God's job and change someone's heart, we only cause frustration to ourselves and pain to the other person.

At another level, often our efforts to change another person are not only futile, but completely mistaken. Sometimes, there is actually nothing wrong with the behavior that bothers us. The person is simply different than we are, which means the problem is in us.

Some people are mechanical, while others are analytical. Some people are outgoing and social, while some are withdrawn and intellectual. Some people are wired to plan and manage, others to live in the moment and respond. Some people enjoy crowds, some people prefer to be alone. All these differences reflect the expansiveness of the creative artistry of the Lord. Next time you're out and about, pay attention to another way that God's artistry is expressed: human noses. He has created billions of them, and each one is different! Or think of the unique timbre of each person's voice. How many people can call you on the phone and, at the moment you hear the voice, you know exactly who it is?

All the myriad differences in our physical makeup and personality hardwiring come from a God of awesome glory who delights in variety. To try to recreate a person in my image is not only futile, but an act of self-deification that seeks to narrow God down to my own width and breadth.

Whether we are trying to change someone's sinful behavior, or to alter someone who has legitimate differences to be more like us, our basic failure is that we do not accept our limits. We fall into believing that we can do what only God can do. The result is never the change we were desiring. All we produce is tension, stress, unhappiness, frustration, discouragement, and hurt.

You Have Limits, You Really Do!

If you are to live productively in this broken-down world, it is absolutely critical that you humbly admit your limits as a human being and then live within them. As we touched on in our discussion of God's sovereignty, the limits on our abilities are extensive and profound. For one thing, because you are a physical being, your life is limited by the laws of the physical universe. The ramifications of this are huge.

You can only be in one place at a time. You can only be in one time at a time: You cannot propel yourself back into the past or launch yourself into the future; your existence is permanently anchored in the here and now.

You cannot think things into existence or alter what has already happened. You cannot remove a conversation from history or redo a disappointing day. You cannot know the details of tomorrow, let alone know exactly where you will be in five years!

You cannot decide you are bored with gravity and want to be free of it. You cannot make a personal commitment to do without oxygen and remain alive. You cannot read or reliably predict the thoughts of another. You cannot control the thoughts, desires, words, or actions of another human being. You cannot keep yourself from aging, as hard as some of us will try.

You cannot release yourself or your surroundings from the affects of the Fall. You cannot assure that your body will be free of disease and sickness. You cannot independently free yourself or another from sin. You cannot reach in and alter the content of your own heart, let alone the heart of another. You cannot plant faith, courage, and hope into the soul of another person. You cannot assure that your government will have integrity or your community will be safe. You cannot make your acquaintances respect you, and you cannot assure that your family members will treat you with love. You cannot keep yourself free from natural and environmental disaster. You cannot control the economic environment, making sure that it does not alter your financial health. You cannot lay out a personal life plan and know it will unfold without interruption. You cannot assure that your life will be easy and satisfying.

When you stand back and consider, you are confronted with how little is actually under your control. When you stop and look, you are faced with your smallness, your weakness, and your limits. But don't get discouraged and don't panic; reality is a healthy place to be. Think about it. Only when I humbly embrace my weakness, humbly admit my limits, and humbly recognize how small I actually am, can I begin to reach out for the help of the loving, powerful, and gracious Redeemer who is the true source of my strength, wisdom, and hope. Only then can I begin to function as an instrument in his powerful hands, rather than being in his way because, in forgetting who I am and who he is, I have been trying to do his job.

You do not have to fear your limits. They were designed by the God who is the definition of everything that is knowledge-able, understanding, wise, and true. Your limits are not a flaw in his creative plan. They are the product of his wise choice and the fulfillment of his intentions. God made you limited, in exactly the way you are.

Yes, you are dependent. No, you are not independently capable. But be very clear on this: your limits are only dangerous when you forget them and try to do things you were never designed to do. When you stay within your limits, you are exactly where God wants you, resting under his perfect, sovereign care. And that is indeed part of their purpose. Your limits are meant to drive you in humble and worshipful need to your Lord for the rescue, restoration, wisdom, and strength only he can give you. And he has promised never to turn a deaf ear to the cry of his children (Psalm 34:15). He has welcomed you to cast your care on him (1 Peter 5:7). He has said that he will never leave you by yourself (Deuteronomy 31:6). Admitting your limits is not a sign of weakness; it is an essential ingredient of mature faith.

Three Inescapable Limits

So, let's take that big laundry list of limits I just named, plus all the ones I didn't name, and bring them down to something a little easier to recall. Every human being is essentially subject to three foundational limits. We are limited in *wisdom*, in *power*, and in *righteousness*. It doesn't take a great deal of humility to agree with this statement, does it? Think of it this way. What would it mean if, in any one of these areas, you were not limited, but unlimited . . . infinite? You really would be the fourth person of the Trinity!

Knowledge and acceptance of these three limits is essential to productive living in this fallen world. What a testimony to our foolish pride that we have any trouble accepting them!

You Have Limited Wisdom

There is so much you and I do not know. There are so many mysteries of the universe that are not yet opened to us. There is so much we have not figured out and do not yet

68

understand. There is so much we think we understand that will be corrected in the future. Our personal field of research and experience is so small.

Almost every day we are bombarded with thoughts, philosophies, perspectives, opinions, viewpoints, explanations, and analyses. Yet we can never make enough time to sift through all we are hearing and experiencing in order to boil it down to what it actually means—to distill knowledge into wisdom. Although we never really stop thinking, because of our limited wisdom our moments of greatest insight are frail, tiny, and imperfect. Paul speaks to our finite understanding when he says, "For the foolishness of God is wiser than man's wisdom, and the weakness of God is stronger than man's strength" (1 Corinthians 1:25). Paul is saying that if God were capable of being foolish, his most foolish moment would be infinitely wiser than your moment of greatest, deepest, fullest insight!

God's understanding has no limits because he has no limits, and he perfectly understands himself. As soon as we acknowledge that our understanding is less than perfect and complete, we acknowledge it is smaller than his to a degree that cannot be measured. Our finiteness is infinitely smaller than his infinity. However much larger than zero our wisdom may be, for all practical purposes it is still nothing when stacked up against his.

In what ways is your understanding limited? In practical terms, it is limited by your experience, your God-given gifts and abilities, the places where you have and have not lived, the people who have mentored and influenced you, and much more. We all simply need to admit that we probably don't know as much as we think we know, whether we're talking about facts or the wisdom to apply them. And we all need to commit ourselves, not only to seeking to know more, but to work to deepen and correct our understanding of the things we think we know. All of us should be aware and afraid of the pride of knowledge. None of us should give way to the smug assurance of arrival. All of us should be living as students, desiring to be truly wise. And all of us would benefit from the commitment to listen more, study more, question more, learn more, and speak less.

But there is another factor we need to humbly accept. Our wisdom is limited by something far more significant than a lack of intellectual capacity. If our mental hard drives were ten times larger and faster, or fifty times, or a thousand times, we would not be ten or fifty or a thousand times wiser. Why? Because, being made in the image of God, we are not merely intellectual beings, as if we were some kind of flesh-based computer. We are moral beings as well, and our moral capacity has been corrupted by sin. Where our intellect merely limits our wisdom, our sinfulness warps and degrades what small wisdom we may actually possess.

No matter how much we know, no matter how wise we are, sin can reduce us all to fools. It is one of sin's most destructive fruits. What is a fool? A fool is one who sees the world upside down and inside out. A fool looks at what is right and sees wrong, and at what is wrong and sees right. A fool looks at what is good and sees bad, and at what is bad and sees good. A fool looks at what is true and thinks it false, and looks at what is false and thinks it true. A fool looks at wisdom and sees foolishness, and looks at foolishness and sees wisdom. Sin does this to all of us. We think our way is better than God's way, that our rules are better than God's rules, and that what we desire is better than what God has promised.

So a man will do whatever it takes to win that argument with his wife, leaving hurt and tension in his wake, rather than giving himself to the patience and love that would result in a relationship of unity and peace. A friend will give run in her heart to bitterness, thinking she can keep it secret and in check, not realizing that her bitterness shapes what she does and says as she relates to her friend. A family will spend themselves into hopeless debt in pursuit of material pleasures. Or a man will give lust room in his heart, yielding to the foolish conceit that he will be able to control it. People will attempt to live outside of a healthy accountability to the body of Christ, thinking they have the maturity to manage their own walk with God. Parents will keep themselves at a level of busyness that prohibits real relationships of love and instruction with their children, only to wonder why those children cause trouble in their teen years. The student gives way to thinking that he can learn and make good grades without discipline and sacrifice, turning his college years into more of a vacation than a time of maturation.

All these are primarily moral failures, not intellectual ones. And somehow, in some way, we all do it. We all step over God's boundaries. We all take our lives into our own hands. We all have had to taste the bitter fruit of our own foolishness. Perhaps the bad fruit is debt, or a damaged relationship, or ill health, or spiritual immaturity, problems that are essentially the result of our foolishness.

When you accept the limits of your wisdom, however, you immediately do two things. First, because you can no longer assume you are as wise as you need to be, you seek true wisdom in the only place it can be found. Here is where Christianity makes one of its most audacious claims. We believe that wisdom isn't first a philosophy or theology. No, we believe that wisdom is a person and his name is Jesus! (See Colossians 2:1–5.) When I come to Christ, I am brought into relationship with the ultimate source of insight, wisdom, understanding, and truth. His wisdom is without comparison and without limits! Ultimately, you don't get wisdom by experience and research; you get wisdom by relationship. God puts his Spirit of Wisdom within you, opening your eyes to see what you never before could have seen, and opening your heart to understand what you could not have previously known. God also gifts you with his Word, which is able to make you wise. In it are revealed all the mysteries of the universe that you must understand in order to live as you were designed to by your Creator.

But there's a second thing you will do as you acknowledge your limited wisdom. Humbly admitting that sin makes you a fool, you will seek rescue and protection. And you will accept that what you need to be protected from is yourself! You will seek the rescue of the ministry of the body of Christ, the rescue of sound worship and faithful biblical preaching, the rescue of good Christian literature, and the rescue of daily personal Bible study and prayer. You will not live as if you have arrived. Your embrace of your daily need for wisdom will open your heart. It will change the way you live.

You Have Limited Power

Suzy comes home from her second grade class one afternoon and says, "Mommy, I have to wear a party dress to school tomorrow." Mom asks, "Is it someone's birthday?" "No," Suzy answers, "We were on the playground and my friend Anna told all the girls that we have to wear party dresses tomorrow." Just two months into second grade, and a girl named Anna is already acting out of a delusion of self-sovereignty. Little Anna has set herself up as Queen of the second-grade playground, basking in her place at the center of her own little universe.

Yes, we all tend to like to be in control. But accepting that there is actually very little in life that we do control is a very important spiritual step. If you buy into the delusion of your own self-sovereignty, if you live committed to some grand plan of your own making, with the belief that you have the independent ability to pull it off, two things will happen. You will not submit your life to the plan of Another, and you won't seek the rest that can only be found in the assurance that God rules over all things for your sake (Ephesians 1:22–23).

Think of the factors that have shaped your life that you had nothing to do with. Think of the location of your birth and how profound an effect it has had. Think of how different things would be had you been born in the jungles of New Guinea, or in the desert of Saudi Arabia, or on some tiny South Sea island. Think of the influence your family has wielded over who you are and how your life has unfolded. You did not choose your mom, your dad, or your siblings, yet each has had a huge effect on you. Think of how profoundly your community and the economy shape your life, when neither operates under your control. Think of how you have never had any actual control over the people in your life. Yes, you can influence them for good or ill, but you cannot make them do what you want. Think of how little control you have had over your own spiritual life. Yes, there was a moment where you had to exercise faith in the sacrifice of Christ, and you have chosen to live as his follower. But you could not have written yourself into the circumstances that exposed you to the things of God, nor could you have opened your own heart to the truth of the gospel.

James calls us to accept the limits of our power with these direct and pastoral words.

> Now listen, you who say, "Today or tomorrow we will go to this or that city, spend a year there, carry on business and make money." Why, you do not even know what will happen tomorrow. What is your life? You are a mist that appears for a little while and then vanishes. Instead, you ought to say, "If it is the Lord's will, we will live and do this or that." As it is, you boast and brag. All such boasting is evil. Anyone, then, who knows the good he ought to do and doesn't do it, sins.
> —James 4:13–17

My security is not to be sought in the degree to which I am able to control the people and situations in my life. No, I can accept the smallness of my power because I am the son or daughter of the King of Kings and Lord of Lords. He is in control, I am not, and that is exactly as it should be.

You Have Limited Righteousness

Does that statement bother you? Actually, it needs to be strengthened. You and I have no independent righteousness at all! All our righteousness has been given to us by Christ. He *is* our righteousness.

It is important to accept the fact that there is never a day in your life that is not somehow stained by sin. Sin rears its ugly head in what you desire, choose, think, say, and do, again and again and again. Nothing that emerges from you is perfectly righteous. You simply are not pure in the true sense of the word.

Yet we are all tempted to buy into the delusion of our own righteousness. Even when our conscience plagues us because we have done something wrong, we try to take ourselves off the hook. We'll tell ourselves that the news about someone, that we just "shared" with a friend, was not gossip, but a prayer request. We'll tell ourselves that that jealous thought was not as envious as it seemed, but was simply a desire for God's blessing. We'll tell ourselves that a selfish play for personal power was really just an expression of our commitment to use our God-given leadership gifts.

If you do not accept your ongoing struggle with sin, if you entertain the thought that your greatest problem in life exists outside of you and not inside, if you try to convince yourself that you are more righteous than you really are, you will not seek the forgiveness and righteousness that can only be found in the Lord Jesus Christ.

Small and Safe

It was a beautiful thing to see. I couldn't stop looking. The setting was a huge and boisterous crowd, mostly men. Probably many of them had had too much to drink. They were coming out of the stadium, celebrating the big win of the home team. There was celebratory grabbing, shoving, and high-fiving all over the place. In the middle of the crowd was a very little boy, just knee-high to many of the men. You would think he would be terrified at that moment, aware of how small he was. You would think that he would be overcome by his limits, but he wasn't. He walked with his head high and a big smile on his face. Why? Because he was with his dad. Wrapped around his little hand was the huge paw of his six-foot-four-inch daddy.

The son kept glancing up at his dad, and in return he kept getting those looks of reassurance that put the smile on his face. I don't think a crowbar could have separated that little boy's hand from his father's. He knew his limits and he knew where security could be found. Surrounded by half-drunk guys several times his size, he was at rest.

Have you placed your little hands in the huge and capable hands of your heavenly Father? Have you realized that your life is played out in the middle of a rowdy and overstimulated crowd? Have you accepted how small you really are? Has that made you panic? Or has it given you rest? You will only ever know the rest God can give you in this broken world when you begin to accept your limits.

You have real and obvious limits to your wisdom, power, and righteousness. But your heavenly Father is infinite in wisdom, and infinite in power, and is the only source of true righteousness. Your God has no boundaries, edges, or limitations. In his power and authority, he bows to no one. You are riddled with imperfections, but God is perfect in every way. Therefore, the key to rest is not in continually lying to yourself in a futile effort to convince yourself you are strong. No, it is when you humbly embrace your foolishness, weakness, and sin that you are in the best position to know peace of heart and to live productively in this broken-down house.

So let your smallness drive you to the One who alone is great. There you will experience that he is not only great in wisdom, power, and holiness. He is also great in grace, and he will give you what you need. It is not your job to be mighty, nor is it within your capacity. That role is reserved for God alone. But like that little boy clinging to his father's hand, you can know what it means to be both small and safe.

Revelation

No
tea leaf lifestyle
trying to read the indicators
hoping to exegete
the past
and divine
the future.
No
hope for the best
blind leaps of faith.
No
Gotta good feeling,
Saw the light.
No
inner peace
God told me.
Don't need a
fortune teller.
No crystal ball
guidance here.
I need revelation
inspired
written
faithful
practical
wise
true,
with a shelf-life
for the ages.
I need something to bank on
something
I can be sure of.

6

Trust What Is Sure

*E*van's life was so unstable and unpredictable that it drove him crazy. The problem was that Evan didn't realize he was the cause. Evan was a Christian. He knew his way around the Scriptures and had a fairly good grasp of theology. But he didn't make much practical use of his Bible. He had a "read the tea leaves" way of dealing with life and seeking direction.

Evan spent an inordinate amount of time trying to figure people out. He was always listening for the words behind the words. He was constantly wondering what people "actually meant" by what they said. He was always analyzing why people did what they did in the way that they did it. He played scenarios over in his head, trying to determine what "really happened." He would call you up after a conversation to ask questions about what you said, why you said it, and if the words meant what he now thought they meant.

The point of all this was to obtain guidance. Evan incessantly picked apart situations in his past, both distant and recent, so he could better predict his future. He was a dedicated archeologist, digging through his personal history in the hope of discovering revelatory gems of understanding that would give him special predictive insight. He was obsessed with knowing what was coming next, and convinced that he needed to know in order to prepare and respond properly.

But most of the time, Evan got it wrong. He wasn't nearly as good at figuring people out as he thought he was, so he was often unprepared for the choices, actions, and words of those around him. He was equally unsuccessful at predicting the future. With all of his analysis, Evan did not have a reliable crystal ball, and usually was not ready for what was coming. His life was unstable because he was basing his decisions and actions on an unreliable body of "insight."

India did not share any of Evan's anxieties. She felt no need to figure it all out. She didn't really care to analyze the people around her, and she surely wasn't about to waste her time trying to divine what would happen next. India lived reactively. She was convinced it was best to "play it cool" and "go with the flow." One small thing: her approach wasn't working, not even a little. The flow hadn't proved too easy to go with, and India's life was a case study in misdirection. She had darted from one boyfriend to another, one job to another, one church to another. She was in debt, unemployed, and almost completely without friends. She was about to be evicted from her apartment and was looking frantically for work.

India saw her life as unfair, and God as distant. She wondered why she was singled out for such a hard road. What India didn't see was how skilled she was at troubling her own trouble.

Everyone lives in a broken world. Everyone lives among flawed people. Everyone is faced with the unpredictable and the unexpected. In this, India was anything but alone. Her problem was that her way of living gave her life no reliable tracks to run on. She was stuck in the mud of it all and didn't know what to do.

A Shocking Diagnosis

When I was in seminary preparing for ministry, I never imagined what I have encountered since then as a counselor. So many times I sat with confused and discouraged people, people who had made regrettable personal decisions that further complicated their travels through this broken world. They would sit with me and wonder aloud why things happened the way they had, and what in the world they should do about it all now. Usually they were hoping there might be some rare, hidden wisdom that would clear things up for them. They craved a revelation, a solution, a magic bullet. And as I listened I would think, *95 percent of what this person is seeking is right there in God's Word.*

These people did not need any new revelation or special insight. They needed to submit to what God had already written. They needed to trust what is sure: the clear words of the Creator of it all, found in the pages of his book, the Bible.

The apostle Paul does a good job in Colossians 2 of diagnosing this endemic problem.

> So then, just as you received Christ Jesus as Lord, continue to live in him rooted and built up in him, strengthened in the faith as you were taught, and overflowing with thankfulness. See to it that no one takes you captive through hollow and deceptive philosophy, which depends on human tradition and the basic principles of this world, rather than on Christ (vv. 6–8).

If you, as a resident of this fallen world, are to follow in the vein of what Paul is teaching here, you must embrace two realities. The first is this: as a person made in the image of God *you do not live life based on the cold, objective facts of your experience, but on your interpretation of your experience.* Everyone living is a philosopher and a theologian. We are always stepping back, taking a look at our lives, and turning our situations and relationships over and over in our hands for further inspection and understanding. The sense you make out of the events of your life will form what you do and say in response to them. As you interpret new events and reinterpret old events, time after time after time, your interpretations will begin to form into a worldview that will function as an organizing structure not only for what you think, but also for how you live.

Here is the second reality: *you are always being bombarded by the opinions of others.* The world around you is not silent. You live in the middle of a constant cacophony of interpretations of reality. Whether it is the opinion of a friend, the lyrics of a song, the words of a text, an article from a newspaper, the plot of a sitcom, some information on a website, or the worldview of a great movie, your eyes are receiving and your mind is being influenced by a thousand voices every day. Each is telling you how to think, and in telling you how to think, is telling you how to live. We never interpret the events of our lives on the basis of pure objectivity; we are always influenced by a myriad of cultural and interpersonal influences.

Now, keep these two realities in mind as you consider Paul's diagnosis. He is saying that Christians, people who really do know the Lord, can be taken captive through "hollow and deceptive philosophy." In this phrase we find a stinging criticism of the limits of human research, experience, and interpretation. Here's what Paul is telling us: Understanding, that is merely human, continually claims that it can provide a reliable basis for daily living, yet it is *hollow* (empty) because it *does not* provide this reliable basis, and it is *deceptive* (false) because it *cannot.* The authoritative truth and wisdom you need to guide you through your situations and relationships simply can't be obtained from any human source.

Then Paul points us to the fatal flaw of human understanding. Such understanding will ultimately fail because it looks to "human tradition and the basic principles of this world" rather than to Christ, "in whom are hidden all the treasures of wisdom and knowledge" (v. 3). This is exactly what made Evan and India's lives so difficult. Each was relying on some basic tradition of human understanding for guidance in daily life. Evan was relying on the power of the human intellect, his own. India was relying on a popular mystical notion she had clearly absorbed somewhere along the line: that a benevolent orderliness in the nature of things will simply guide you into goodness. Both of them had forgotten about the Fall, about the reality of this broken-down house of a universe.

Human "wisdom" that cannot be aligned with Scripture simply is not wisdom at all. Because Evan and India had embraced fallen imitations of wisdom, they lived stressful and disappointing lives full of unexpected problems and confusion. They had been taken captive and didn't know it, even as they held in their hands the only truly reliable source of understanding and direction: the Word of God, written guidance from the One who supplies every treasure, insight, wisdom, and truth.

Watching Your Feet

So, more than six billion people on this planet are trying to navigate through an increasingly interconnected world of spiritual confusion and moral weakness. Is this all the fault of Adam and Eve's sin? Not really. Even in their sinless garden, the first man and woman were not equipped to figure out life on their own. We know this because God immediately began to speak to them and direct them, as soon as they were created and before the serpent ever uttered a word. By themselves, Adam and Eve would have had no idea who they were or why they existed; no idea how to spend their days. So we see that from the very beginning we were created to be dependent on God, to be willing listeners and humble receivers. God's Word, spoken directly to man, would give us sure and certain guidance.

Now, if this was true of Adam and Eve before sin entered the world, how much more true is it of you and me, who have never known a single sinless day, and are constantly bombarded by unbiblical messages from the world? Certainly, we need to be careful to trust in what we can be sure of.

No passage gets at this need and God's provision better than Psalm 119:105. "Your word is a lamp to my feet and a light for my path." When do you need a lamp? Well, you probably wouldn't pack a flashlight for a picnic lunch in the park. But you wouldn't think of taking that nighttime walk through the woods without one. And which scenario is more like life in this fallen world: a picnic lunch, or midnight in the woods? You must not try to live as if life is a sunny afternoon picnic. Sin has plunged your world into darkness. On any given day you probably encounter far more falsehood than you do truth. So if you are going to move forward, to make your way without danger, and get to where you are meant to go, you need something to light your way.

You need light for your marriage and your parenting. You need light for your job and your relationships with your neighbors. You need light for your struggles with desires and temptations. You need light to help you deal with the unexpected. You need light to cope with new difficulties that emerge. You need light for when you have been sinned against. You need light to deal with weaknesses of the body and hardships of the heart. You need light for those moments when you're alone and overwhelmed. You need light for all those unknowns that will show up on your doorstep tomorrow, the day after tomorrow, and for the rest of your life.

You don't need to bloody your nose and bruise your toes by bumping into trees and tripping over roots. You don't have to grope around fearfully in the darkness. The Light of the World has graced you with the light of his Word. It will shine around your feet in the midst of the darkness so you need not stumble and fall. Listen to the reflections of that great nineteenth century preacher, Charles Spurgeon, on this passage.

> Thy word is a lamp unto my feet. We are walkers through the city of this world, and we are often called to go out into its darkness; let us never venture there without the light giving word, lest we slip with our feet. Each man should use the word of God personally, practically, and habitually, that he may see his way and see what lies in it. When darkness settles down upon all around me, the word of the Lord, like a flaming torch, reveals my way. Having no fixed lamps in eastern towns, in old time each passenger carried a lantern with him that he might not fall into the open sewer, or stumble over the heaps of ordure which defiled the road. This is a true picture of our path through this dark world: we should not know the way, or how to walk in it, if Scripture, like a blazing flambeau, did not reveal it. One of the most practical benefits of Holy Writ is guidance in the acts of daily life: it is not sent to astound us with its brilliance, but to guide us by its instruction. It is true the head needs illumination, but even more the feet need direction, else head and feet may both fall into a ditch. Happy is the man who personally appropriates God's word, and practically uses it as his comfort and counsellor,—a lamp to his own feet. (Charles Spurgeon, *Treasury of David*)

Prepared Spontaneity

Wise people are not wise because they are prophets who see the future. Wise people are not wise because they can look into men's hearts and discern their thoughts and motives. Wise people are not wise because they are better at learning from experience. Wise people are not those who have been blessed with superior intellect.

Wise people are those who treasure the lamp of God's Word, seeking out and crying out for the light of truth. In other words, wise people are simply prepared people—biblically prepared and equipped for whatever might come along. People become wise when by God's grace they are humble enough to accept how unprepared they actually are in themselves. Sacrificing the false god of their own independence, they run to the one place where actual certainty can be found. Then they are able to live hopefully, productively, and courageously. Then they are prepared for whatever comes along—not because they saw it coming, but because they have been students of the Word of God. They don't know more about the future than anyone else does. But God, through the wisdom of the Bible, has made them ready for it.

In one sense, this is the secret of "going with the flow" that India thought she was pursuing. In the light of Scripture, however, the nature of all that going and flowing is completely different. It is not passive. It is grounded in truth, it understands the real nature of this existence, and it is active and attentive.

I call this the principle of *prepared spontaneity*. You do not need God-like powers to live a God-honoring life in this fallen world. The perspectives, commands, principles, and promises of the great redemptive story of Scripture will provide all you need to live as you were designed to live; yes, even in this broken world.

You can respond spontaneously and biblically to a myriad of things you did not see coming because God's Word makes you wise about you, about others, about the meaning and purpose of life, about God and his plan, about basic rights and wrongs, about why things are the way they are and what to do about it, about how we function and how change takes place, and about a host of other things. And because the Bible has made you wise, you are then ready to face what you neither planned nor expected. You are ready because you are trusting in what is sure rather than reading the tea leaves of your own viewpoint or passively going with the flow.

Broken House, Skilled Builder

Understanding and practicing prepared spontaneity can indeed enable you to live productively for God, but I'm not for a minute suggesting life will never be hard again. Every situation, location, and relationship of our everyday lives is in some way broken. As fallen creatures, the best we can ever do in this life is know *how* to live in a broken-down house; nothing and no one but God himself, in the fullness of his time, can change *where* we live. So, as we experience the reality of life in this house, sometimes it will leave us confused and overwhelmed. Sometimes it will leave us hurt and angry. Sometimes we will give way to envy because the house of someone living nearby seems far less broken. Sometimes we will just get weary of the stress of it all and long for a house in perfect repair.

In those moments, those days, those seasons, remember that you are never on your own. The Builder has given you a copy of his repair manual, the Bible. It will help you understand why things are as broken as they are. It will teach you how to live well even in the midst of the brokenness. And it will explain the only way in which repair can ever happen. More than that, the Builder himself has moved into the house with you. You have not been left alone. You can rest assured of his presence and his wisdom. His grace has gifted you with both of these.

He who offers you such grace and guidance will never ask you to do what you are not fully capable of doing by God's grace and indwelling Spirit. He will not demand things of you that are beyond your abilities. Your Lord is tender and kind. He knows who you are and he knows where you are living. He knows how hard it is to live in this broken-down house because in the flesh he lived here himself. He invites you to walk away from trying to figure it out on your own and he welcomes you to sit at his feet and learn the mysteries of the universe; things so profound that you will see your world in a radically new way; things so practical that you will never live the same way again.

You are never in a better place than when you give up on you and begin to trust what is sure: the life-shaping wisdom of the One who built the house in the first place.

A Matter of the Heart

Remember Israel,
on the way to make
sacrifice
to Jehovah,
they stopped and did
homage
to Baal.
Remember Judas,
he attended the supper
after he
sold
Jesus for a little
Silver.
Remember the Pharisees,
so publicly
committed
yet they plotted Jesus'
death.
What seems
so very spiritual
on the surface
may not be
in reality
a matter of the
heart.

7

Resist Spirituality

Are you confused or offended by the title of this chapter? Are you thinking, "But hasn't God called me to pay attention to spirituality?" Permit me to tell you a story.

His was one of those dramatic testimonies we have all heard about. He had been the tough kid, from the rough family. He was street-smart and could read people well. But he crossed paths with the law one too many times and ended up paying the price. While in jail, he was visited by someone involved in prison ministry, an equally tough guy with an amazing story who loved to talk.

It wasn't long before he was looking forward to visits from the "Jesus guy." And the more he listened, the more the message he was hearing made sense. Parole came quickly. Once out, he moved into the neighborhood where his new-found friend lived and began to attend his church. He couldn't believe how he was welcomed with open arms. He quickly realized that people loved to hear him tell his story. He told it to his small group, to the men's ministry, and to the youth group. He was even invited to tell his story at a women's luncheon.

He learned his lessons well, and became both biblically and theologically literate. He joined the church's prison ministry and soon was running it. He led a small group, went on short-term mission trips, and even led a few himself. He could debate theology with the best of them and always seemed ready to do so. He was soon an elder overseeing men's ministries in the church. With his wife of four years and two young children, his story looked like a case study in transforming grace.

But there were some things that didn't seem to fit. He was not known for being a servant. It really did seem as though he had to be in control of everything he touched. He was also known for having a short fuse; everyone around him had experienced his anger at some point. Even though he was always in leadership, he never had a stable church life. After several months, or a year or two, he would become critical of the direction of the church and transfer his family's membership elsewhere.

Things blew up one Thursday night in an ugly argument with his wife when he admitted to an adulterous affair. This wasn't a heartfelt confession leading to repentance, but an arrogant announcement that he had found "a better woman." He did not respond well to his pastors as they sought to provide the assistance and intervention of solid biblical counsel. In fact, he threatened to take legal action if they didn't back off. The decisions that followed had the look of a man who was in the process of forsaking the faith.

Christless Christianity

In telling this story, I have in mind an actual person. But if I were to alter the details a little, I could tell a dozen more stories that are strikingly similar and equally real. How do you make sense of such a life? How do you understand an apparent conversion that ends up this way? It looked like this man's life had been completely turned around. So, what happened here? And why?

This is where the words of John can help us. "They went out from us, but they did not really belong to us. For if they had belonged to us, they would have remained with us; but their going showed that none of them belong to us" (1 John 2:19).

The more attuned your ears are to the politically correct language of the world, the more difficult it can be to receive this blunt, tell-it-like-it-is passage from John. But I am persuaded that there are indeed many people in Christian churches who are very similar to our friend the ex-convict. And I am convinced this is caused by a cruel trick of the enemy, with the unwitting cooperation of well-meaning Christians.

This side of heaven, we must resist defining spirituality as anything other than a deep devotion to Christ, the fruit of which is a lifestyle of daily worship of him and active service in his kingdom. We must be keenly aware of the covert danger of a Christless Christianity which passes itself off as something it is not, and in so doing, has the power to deceive and derail many. Christless Christianity gives false assurance of salvation, and when those who possess it "go out from us," it can fill true believers with doubt and confusion.

This covert war must be fought within our churches, in the power and love of the gospel, until Christ returns. We must be sure that the spirituality we teach and live is the true spirituality of the Bible, not an externalistic counterfeit that omits Christ.

This means that we cannot be satisfied with a faith that lives most vibrantly in abstract theological concepts and the ease of Sunday-morning services. We cannot be satisfied with a Christianity that features episodic moments of ministry but otherwise is shaped by the values of the world. We cannot be satisfied with a Christianity that simply fills another slot in an all-too-busy schedule. We cannot be satisfied with a Christianity that allows us to live at the center of our world. We cannot be satisfied with a Christianity that does not live the biblical hymns we sing and does not apply the biblical exhortations we have heard.

Self-righteous, self-satisfied, and externalistic spirituality is dangerous and must be resisted. It is not a by-product of true conversion, but flows from the man-centeredness of secular thinking. It is the house of self all dressed up to look like the house of God. This is what makes it so dangerous; it has an amazing ability to look and feel like the real thing.

John makes it clear that those who truly "walk away from" faith in Christ actually never had such faith to begin with. Theirs was a Christless Christianity. They were not converts, not in possession of authentic biblical faith. I'll say it again: I believe many of our churches implicitly and unintentionally teach a false spirituality that fosters such inauthentic faith. This false spirituality promotes new false conversions, masks existing false conversions—often for years—and cripples the life effectiveness of genuine believers by causing them to lose focus and direction.

True Humanity
When God draws us to himself, he is not calling us to develop some separate dimension of our lives called "spirituality." No, he is calling us to offer every aspect and every dimension of our lives to him; living as if he really is at the center of everything we are and have. True spirituality is not about doing a bunch of new things (although that will happen). True spirituality is about doing everything we do for a new *purpose*, and because of this new purpose, in a new *way*. True spirituality is about submitting to God what in the past I had always kept back for myself. It is about realizing that his grace rescues me from *me* precisely by motivating and empowering me to live a life of devotion to *him*.

In this way, *the grace of Christ actually returns to me my humanity*. What do you think was meant to character-ize authentic human living? What was the original (and still unchanged) purpose of human existence? That our lives might revolve around service to God and love of others. In practical, tangible ways, my life ought to demonstrate devotion to God and a self-sacrificing love of others. If it is not, I am living neither in authentic Christianity nor in true humanity. True spirituality is inseparable from the stuff of daily life, and inseparable from true humanity. I am never more authentically human than when I am living in functional worship of God and active love for my neighbor.

Characteristics of a Counterfeit

Let's look more closely now at how false spirituality can point us away from Christ. Here are five common ways in which counterfeit faith goes wrong.

It Mistakes Commitment to Christianity for Commitment to Christ

The systems, traditions, locations, institutions, sights, sounds, and culture of Christianity are engaging and exciting, and they should be. The danger is that they can actually function as a replacement for a relationship with Christ. You see this dynamic at work in Christ's parable of the Pharisee and the tax collector (see Luke 18:9–14). Although the Pharisee was a religious man and was in the temple praying, his prayer was not an act of relationship with and submission to God. If you pay attention to the content of the prayer, the Pharisee, so convinced of his righteousness, was actually announcing to God that he did not need him.

It is possible to mistake identity in Christianity for identity in Christ. I can serve and enjoy the externals of Christianity more than I serve and enjoy Christ. I can and should take pleasure in my inclusion in the *culture of Christianity*. But that must ever and always take a back seat to the daily rescue and help I receive because of my inclusion in the *grace of Christ*.

It Mistakes Bible Knowledge for Biblical Wisdom

It is quite possible to grow in Bible knowledge without growing in holiness or wisdom. Having worked for twenty years at one of the finest seminaries in the world, I have seen this happen again and again. The students at this seminary are put through a rigorous theological curriculum. They are taught how to think their way through all the essential issues of their faith. Yet I have had scores of third-year seminarians, just a few months from graduation, seek my counsel because they have lived unwisely during their seminary years and are now harvesting the fruit of their foolishness.

It is scary, but true. Knowledge and foolishness can live together, even though it seems they shouldn't be able to. Wisdom is something deeper than intellectual comprehension. Wisdom is something you live. You don't show wisdom by demonstrating what you know. You reveal wisdom by the way you think, desire, choose, act, react, speak, and respond to the situations and relationships around you.

It Mistakes Commitment to a System of Theology and Rules for Christian Maturity

If your Christianity is something less than a surrender of the thoughts and motives of your heart to the Lordship of Jesus Christ, and a daily hunger for and pursuit of his transforming grace, then your Christianity will tend to get reduced to a system of theology and rules. Now, I love the theology of the Word of God and I am very thankful for the wisdom, insight, and protection of God's law. But if all we needed was an ideology and an ethic, Jesus would never have had to come!

It is dangerous to define Christian maturity by how biblically literate and theologically knowledgeable a person has become. It is dangerous to reduce biblical maturity to how well you keep to a list of rules. This was the kind of spirituality God so vehemently rejected in the Old Testament. (See Isaiah chapters 1 and 29; particularly 29:13.) The grace of Christ has been given to transform me at the level of the deepest, most profound motives, thoughts, desires, purposes, perspectives, and cravings of my heart. Christianity that does not promote a spirituality of the heart is not true biblical Christianity. (See the Sermon on the Mount, Matthew 5–7.)

It Mistakes Doing New "Religious" Things for a Heart of Obedience to Christ

Sometimes, what looks like obedience on the surface may not be obedience at all. Permit me two examples that will ring true for many parents. You ask your child to turn off his Gameboy and go clean his room. As he goes down the hallway he loudly and rather disrespectfully complains about your request. If obedience is a willing submission of the heart to the authorities God has placed in his life, then this child is not being obedient. No, what looks a little like external obedience is not obedience at all, but a rebellious heart bowing only reluctantly to the power of another. Or your teenager debates with you the exact words you recently used in asking her to do something. She is not exegeting your vocabulary out of a heart that delights in obedience. No, she is legalistically deconstructing your words in search of some loophole through which she can step to freedom.

In the same way, my involvement with the meetings and ministries of my local church may not be acts of willing obedience at all. They may simply be part of a system of penance and self-atonement, efforts to ease my conscience about the fact that I really do live as if my life belongs to me. It could also be that I value my church membership for cultural or personal reasons, so I "serve" that I might be seen as a member in good standing. The first turns my church participation into a particularly ineffective form of therapy. The second reduces me to being a member of a club, rather than a participant in an ongoing celebration of God's grace and a servant who makes willing sacrifices for the sake of God's kingdom.

It Mistakes Participation in Ministry Opportunities for a Christlike Lifestyle

It is good and proper for the local church to design, organize, and schedule various ministries for the body of Christ. But the call of Christ for me is to offer every aspect of my life to him for his service, not just those my church emphasizes.

This means I cannot be satisfied with a way of thinking about ministry that allows separation between life and ministry. To step out of my life into some episodic moment of ministry and then step back into a non-ministry mode ought to feel strange. Under that model, you see, most of my life is still retained, owned, and ruled by me. But true Christianity is characterized by a "total involvement" paradigm of ministry: all of God's people, all of the time. Life as ministry, and ministry as life.

I am not to think of my life as separate from ministry, nor am I to think of ministry as separate from my life. I am to give myself to a way of living that views every dimension of human life as a forum for ministry. I don't live with a willingness to occasionally minister. I am not "open to ministry opportunities." No, I commit myself to live with a ministry mentality where my actions, reactions, and responses are more shaped by a desire to be part of what God is doing on earth than to fulfill my personal wants and needs.

I don't know about you, but I see the seeds of all these tendencies in my own walk with God. I do tend to want a Christianity free of personal sacrifice. I do want to control my own world. I do want to follow the Lord *and* live for my own pleasure. I do grumble in the face of the Lord's call. There are times I would rather have an external spirituality than a Christianity that offers the rulership of my heart to God.

Too Easily Satisfied

As I noted earlier, I am persuaded that the problem with the body of Christ is not that we are dissatisfied with what we do not have, but that we are all too satisfied with what we do have. We are comfortable with a little bit of holiness, a little bit of ministry, a little bit of sacrifice, a little bit of wisdom, a little bit of the satisfying glory that only the grace of Christ is able to give us. I am deeply persuaded that we must resist with all of our might the kind of self-satisfied spirituality that marks the life of so many believers. And I am further persuaded that this pseudo-spirituality is one of the cruel deceptions of a wily enemy.

What is the danger of this kind of spirituality? It never results in truly Christ-centered, grace-driven, God-glorifying, heart-satisfying righteousness. True righteousness only ever begins when you come to the end of yourself. Only when God leads you to the place where you begin to abandon your own agenda and false righteousness, does true righteousness take hold. And only then can a passion for selfless service and true worship begin to grow in your heart.

But the battle is ever-present, and I am afraid that at the same moment we are nibbling at the table of the Lord, we are often stuffing ourselves at the buffet of the world. No wonder our hearts are not satisfied; we are feasting on food that has no capacity to satisfy. And no wonder we are addicted; as we feed on what cannot satisfy, we must go back again and again and again.

You live in a fallen world. The temptation is everywhere. It's hard not to love the world and the things that are in the world. It's hard to love an invisible God more than the visible things that surround you. It's hard not to offer God a few pieces of your life while retaining most of it for yourself. It's hard not to reduce your walk with God down to a formal, external religion that lays no claim to the interior of your life. It's hard to grasp that you actually have to die before you can live. It's hard to grasp that your life is no longer your own.

It's equally hard to grasp that until the day we die, we are called to engage in battle. Yet that is the only way to resist temptation. The effective counterweight to the continual, relentless pull away from vibrant faith is a Spirit-empowered, grace-motivated spiritual war fought in our hearts every day. True spirituality recognizes the presence of this war, and recognizes that the Lord is your captain and fights on your behalf. Yet such genuine spirituality is also willing to fight the good fight of faith, day after day after day, proactively, in the gracious strength God supplies.

You have been called to resist. You are daily given the grace to resist. Jesus took your punishment so you could be free to confess your externalism and know you will receive forgiveness and help. Are you resisting a Christless Christianity? Are you resisting a spirituality that is not a matter of the heart? Do you no longer want to be satisfied with just a few morsels from the Lord's banquet table? And are you humbly crying out for the grace that has been given for just this struggle?

Eavesdrop on Eternity

Now,
so visible
so powerful
so compelling.
See
hear
taste
touch
measure
quantify
acquire
possess
serve.
I need
values
perspective
direction
purpose
deliverance from
the magnetic draw
of here and now.
I need to
eavesdrop on eternity.

8

Listen to Eternity

*J*oan had real hope. Not because her life was easy. In fact, the unthinkable had happened and things weren't about to get much better anytime soon. For a while there, before everything fell apart, it really looked as though she had it all. But now that seemed like ages ago. And even though she was far worse off in the world's eyes, she was right where she wanted to be. Joan was grateful. She trusted God. She had hope.

Years earlier, before I met her, Joan had come to Christ and met and married Henry, a successful, wealthy Christian businessman. They built a mansion in one of those affluent suburbs so many people dream of living in. They had a circle of great Christian friends and were involved together in several exciting ministry projects. As the years zipped by, Joan gave birth to three healthy and vibrant children. All in all, there was little she lacked.

It wasn't a big deal at first, but in the little moments she began to notice two things about Henry. He seemed distant; not as communicative. Well, he was a busy man. The other thing got her attention even more. Henry seemed to be at the edge of irritation and anger all the time. Joan tried her best to avoid things that would upset him, and she told herself that he was under stress because of his rapidly expanding business, but in her heart of hearts she knew there was more.

She was right. Before long the relationship morphed into a state of uncomfortable marital détente. They talked only when schedule or finances demanded it. He increasingly was an absentee husband, often coming home only after she had gone to bed. Joan tried to talk to him about the distance between them, but he always shut down the conversation by angrily reminding her of the great life he had given her.

In desperation, she began to seek help for her marriage. She wanted solid advice before she approached Henry again. But it wasn't long before she was meeting with me alone. Henry wouldn't come. He was convinced she was the one who really needed help. Again and again I tried to reach out to Henry, but he only seemed to get angrier.

Hurt, frustrated, and exhausted, Joan decided to get away for a weekend with two of her closest friends. She needed a break, she needed to clear her head and decide what to do next, and she needed the encouragement these women could give her. She looked forward to the weekend and was relieved as they headed down the road to the lake-front house they had rented. She had no idea what was happening back at her home.

For eighteen months, Henry had been expertly planning his exit. He had divested himself of the company, putting all his assets in the name of his partner. He not only wanted to get out, he wanted to devastate Joan, both emotionally and financially. As Joan's anger had grown during the past six months, it only increased Henry's desire to hurt her. The trucks were at the house less than half an hour after Joan drove away.

Arriving back home late Sunday night, rounding a curve in the long, majestic driveway, the first thing Joan noticed was that the house was completely dark. She wouldn't really expect anyone to be awake at this hour, but . . . no lights at all? Stepping from her car and walking toward the front door, she was trying to rationalize it. But it all felt very wrong, and fear rose in her throat.

Inside, she found the switch by the door, and the great space filled with light. Joan gasped, cried, and screamed all at the same time. The sound bounced off blank walls, empty floors, and uncovered windows. She ran through the house, hysterically yelling the names of her children, but all she encountered was room after empty, echoing room. There was still one bed. In the kitchen was one small table. Her personal possessions were left in closets or dumped in a few boxes. Everything else was gone.

She sat on the floor in the empty family room and, despite the hour, desperately called friend after friend. Of those who answered, no one knew a thing. Her mind raced and her heart pounded, but she could make no sense out of what was happening. She called Henry again and again. None of his numbers were working.

She found the note on a cold granite countertop in the kitchen: Henry was never coming back; he would give her visitation rights to see the children if she didn't make trouble for him, but she was going to have to fend for herself. Joan tore up the note, ran upstairs, threw herself on the bed, and began to cry. She woke up Monday with her eyes hurting and called me. I couldn't make much sense of her frightened, confused sentences, but we decided to meet later that day.

Dangerous Hope

The first thing Joan said to me that afternoon was, "I have lost all hope." I understood what she was saying and why. You see, for a long time Joan's hope had been a dangerous hope. It was hope in a man, hope in material things, hope in a house, hope in a family, and hope in a lifestyle. Now, there is nothing inherently wrong with appreciating people or position or possessions. But these temporal things were never designed to be a source of hope. To hope in temporal things is to hope in what I cannot control and what is not guaranteed to me.

Joan had built her house on sinking sand and she didn't even know it. Yes, she was a Christian, but Christ was not for her the source of that inner sense of well-being every person desires. She had staked her life on a man and a collection of things and now all of it was gone and she simply didn't know how to think or what to do.

She had been left penniless. Henry was still going to their church, but he had poisoned many of her closest friends against her, so she was almost friendless and couldn't face going to meetings. She didn't know where her children were, and it would take a long and expensive court battle even to try to get them back.

Joan was facing some of the harshest and most hurtful realities of life in this broken world, and there was no escape. The things she had looked to for her daily support had all vanished, and her life would never be the same. It was one of those profoundly discouraging times where death really does seem easier than life. What could she do? How would she ever face life again? How would she ever be able to hope again? It all seemed so overwhelming, so impossible. She had lived so long in comfort and ease, having no idea whatsoever that her world of hope was about to explode.

Standing

I will never forget the afternoon, weeks later, when I got another call from Joan. She was still alone. Materially, she had next to nothing. She was living off government assistance as she took a class that would enable her to support herself.

She had seen her children only twice since Henry left. Most of her dearest friends had melted away under the heat of what she was dealing with every day. I picked up the ringing phone and, without even identifying herself she said exuberantly, "I'm standing!" Her words echoed in my mind as a sure sign of the transforming power of God through his Word. She had hope; firm, unwavering, and reliable hope. Her heart was no longer a place of torment. Fear had given way to courage. Despair had given way to joy. Death was no longer an attractive escape.

What had happened to Joan, and what produced these changes, was simple yet profound. Joan had done something she had never done before. She had begun to embrace one of the most radical realities of a biblical worldview. This is a perspective so shocking, so outrageous, and so hard to envision, that we tend to wall it off in the "theologically interesting but basically irrelevant" area of our brains. Yet it is the only thing that really brings any sense to what God calls us to be. If you live in light of this reality it will alter the way you think about yourself and everything around you. It will give you reason to build your life around and commit your resources to the things you have been called to do. It can literally change the way you feel about everything. Far from being esoteric or impractical, it is one of the biblical realities that make life in this sin-shattered world livable.

Joan began to listen to eternity. And when she did, she got her hope back.

Listening to eternity helps us know how to live in the here and now. We cannot understand what is truly important, or grasp the reality of what we face in this life, or know what to do about it, until we see life from the perspective of eternity. A biblical view of eternity brings the Christian genuine hope in any situation, and hope produces insight and courage. The Bible invites us to listen in and learn so that, in this broken world of bitter hurt and disappointment, we may find hope.

What in the World Is Hope?

Joan's original hope had failed her because it wasn't reliable. It was just a dreamy wish for things that can slip from our grasp at any moment. But true hope is a confident expectation of a guaranteed result. This kind of hope has roots in something solid, unchangeable, everlasting. It has roots in eternity. In 1 Corinthians, Paul makes two powerful points about eternity: it is necessary for our faith to make sense, and it should change how we live.

Christianity Makes No Sense without Eternity

Listen to Paul's words. "If only for this life we have hope in Christ, we are to be pitied more than all men" (1 Corinthians 15:19). The love, the obedience, the sacrifice, and the worship that we are called to in the here and now make no sense without an eternity. If all we have is this life, then what comes next is . . . nothing. Take that view, and the name of the game is to get as much comfort, pleasure, control, and power as possible, right now.

But that is not how we are called to live. Everything God calls us to do with our hearts and our hands looks to the sure reality of an eternity. Now is but a brief preparation for the forever that is on the other side.

Paul made this argument to people who thought there was no such thing as resurrection. Based on that view, they claimed that not even Christ had been raised. Paul replied that if Christ is not raised, our faith is vain, because there is no defeat of the suffering, sin, and death that pervade our world. Without resurrection, life ends at the final breath, and we are merely machines. But the promise of eternity is ultimate victory over all sin, suffering, and death. The resurrection of Jesus guarantees that these things have been defeated, and that we too will rise and live forever in a place free of them. But there is more.

Eternity Changes How We Think About "Now"

Here is the logic. If Christ conquered sin and death in his resurrection, thereby guaranteeing eternal life, then the question is "What is going on *here*, in *this* life?" Well, Paul tells us. "For he must reign until he has put all his enemies under his feet. The last enemy to be destroyed is death" (1 Corinthians 15:25–26).

This means that our world is not one of chance and chaos. It is a world under the personal rule of a Redeemer who is so loving that he willingly gave his life for others, and so powerful that he is able to defeat even death. Think of how radical this is. You are never alone in your relationships and circumstances. Your world is inhabited by a powerful and living Redeemer who is at work collecting all the spoils of his victory on your behalf. Evil is in the process of being defeated. Death will eventually die. There is reason for hope even when your life has fallen down around your feet. Change really is possible because of Christ's rule. Real victory is possible. Justice and mercy will win!

The Sound of Eternity

So, what about Joan?

No, Joan's husband never came back, and her kids suffered from the shattering of their parents' marriage. Joan lost most of her friends permanently and will probably struggle with her finances for many years to come. But in the middle of it all something wonderful happened. Joan got hope like she had never had it before—a hope that will never shame her or let her down.

Joan began to listen to eternity. She finally realized that the guarantee of her hope was not to be found in the size of her house or bank account. It was not to be found in her circle of friends. It was not to be found in the love of a man or in her work as a mother. Hope was to be found in what the empty tomb of Jesus Christ guaranteed her.

Joan discovered huge comfort in embracing the fact that what is, will not always be. There will come an eternal day without betrayal or injustice. There will come an everlasting day without anger or vengeance. There will come a day when no more pain ever fills the heart and no more tears ever fill the eyes. But with all this hope of future comfort, Joan was not merely being called to wait. No, she was being called to see "now" in a very different way.

Joan started to rest in the fact that the world she awakes to each day is a world under rule. Her world is guided by One who is working out his plan. She lives in a world where the enemies of God and good are being progressively defeated. She sees that even in the hurt and confusion of difficulty and disappointment, you can have hope because Jesus is reigning. He will make sure that evil is defeated and that every promise he made is fulfilled. Because Jesus conquered death, life is not impossible or futile. Rather, he is bringing his work to a certain conclusion, and he will reign forever.

As Joan listened to eternity, something else happened. She began to pay attention in a new way to the words of saints who had passed over to the other side. She listened to what they said and she learned. "Salvation belongs to our God, who sits on the throne, and to the Lamb" (Revelation 7:10b). When these saints look back, they don't say, "We lived in the best house!" Or, "We wore the best clothes!" Or, "We ate the finest food!" Or, "We had the most wonderful marriage!" Or, "Life was so pleasurable and comfortable!" No, as fitting as it is to be thankful for all these things, this is not what fills the hearts of saints in eternity. From the vantage point they have been given, they have a crystal-clear sense of what is most important. They have their values right, and in Scripture we are given a glimpse of what *they* consider central so we don't have to wait until we join them there to get *our* values right.

Looking back, Joan realized that for all the material comfort and trappings of success, so much of her life had been a frenetic attempt to keep her world together. She had thought life was to be found in her family, home, friendships, and possessions. But the house was never quite right. The kids never seemed to measure up to her expectations. Henry was never quite able to please her. Her friends were never quite loyal enough. The finances were never quite secure enough. She never even met her own expectations. Because she had placed her hope in this physical world, she needed it to be perfect. But it was not perfect. It was terribly broken by sin.

The things of this world were never designed to contain hope or to give life. When Joan's world fell apart and her false assurances were exposed, she felt her life was over. But since then, Joan has listened and learned. As a result, she lives with hope and courage she had never before known. There are still days when she feels anxiety for the future and misses the material ease of her past. There will probably always be a bit of an ache in her heart over what once was. But with it all is a persistent joy, freedom, and rest she had desired for years.

Joan's life had been one of unrealistic expectations, endless demands, and constant worry. But, in a powerful demonstration of where life is and is not to be found, God liberated Joan from all of that. And in the middle of her grief, Joan did the one thing that she had needed to do for a very long time. She began to listen to eternity. When she did, her approach to life changed as radically as it had when she first believed.

Are You Listening?

What about you? Are you asking people, circumstances, and things to do what they were never designed to do? Are there ways in which you look to this fallen world to become your own personal messiah? At the street level, the heart level, where you live every day, what really does carry your hope?

Are you working frantically to secure hope that you simply do not have the personal power to secure?

When you come to the end of a day or a week and pronounce it "good," what made it good? What is it that you are asking your situations and relationships to give you? Are you happy? Fulfilled? Content? Secure? Restful? Appreciative? Satisfied? If so, why? And if not, why not? What holds your hope?

I think I will never forget my final conversation with Joan. I was asking her how she was doing and what she had learned. She said the most remarkable thing. "You know, Paul, I hope that I never have to go through again what I have been through over the last three years, but I am very thankful for this experience and what I have learned. I can't believe that I was one of God's children and yet I lived for so many years without hope. God had to remove all of the things that were giving me false hope so that I could finally experience where true hope is to be found."

I wanted to be sure I had heard her correctly, so I asked her to repeat it. Yes, she was actually thankful for having suffered something that, at one time, even to imagine it would have been deeply troubling. That's something only grace can do!

So I ask you again. Are you listening? Are you listening to the eternity that is your hope? Are you listening for the sounds of victory and words of triumph? Are you listening to the promises for the here and now—promises of a rule that guarantees that every other promise the Ruler has made to you is trustworthy and sure? Can it be said of you that, because you have listened, you know where to look for hope, you know what is important, and you are no longer anxious?

Joan had seen every shred of her false hope stripped away. In its place she was given true hope more real, precious, and lasting than any other. She listened and learned and she will never be the same again. Someday Joan—and you and I—will be there on the other side. She will no longer mourn what she has lost, but she will say with her fellow pilgrims, now finally home, "Salvation belongs to our God, and to the Lamb!" And she will know then, as never before, that the hope she got in those dark days of loss never did disappoint her.

Wait

I have come to
understand
that I am not the
author
of my own story.
My narrative
is being penned
by One
who is the definition
of all that is
wise
loving
pure
true
and good.
But since I am
in the story but not the
author of the story
I am often called
to wait.
I wish I could say
that I wait well
but I don't.
I wish I could say
that I never question
your wisdom
but I do.

So, Lord
once more I ask for the
grace to wait
not only so I can get
what I'm waiting for
but so that I will become
what you want me to become
as I wait.

9
Learn to Wait

I am not very good at it. In fact, I find it to be one of the most difficult disciplines of life in this fallen world. How can something that sounds like doing nothing be so hard to do well? Yet it is hard. It is also inescapable. God calls each of us to wait.

How well do you wait? Perhaps it is all the mundane little moments that get under your skin. Maybe you hate the lines at the grocery store, or the crawling traffic of your morning routine. Maybe you're exhausted just waiting for your children to grow up. Or perhaps you're tired of waiting for the hard work of your career to pay off. Perhaps it's the long, drawn-out pain of waiting for your marriage to change, or for that person to own up to how much he or she has hurt you. Maybe you're just tired of waiting through the myriad little difficulties that each day in this broken world seems to hold.

Your circumstances will be different than mine, but we will both face plenty of waiting in this life, and God has a purpose in every second of it. So it's worth taking a look at this shared calling, that we might understand it better and practice it more effectively. We begin with the story of Maria and Chad.

Maria was called to wait in a very hard place, her marriage. She had dreamed that she and Chad would have a wonderful life, raising their children and growing old together. In the beginning it seemed like Maria was getting her dream. Before she and Chad were married, they had been virtually inseparable. They shared the same perspectives on life, they enjoyed the same activities, and they both took their relationship with Christ very seriously. Contrary to popular warnings, their first year of marriage went smoothly. They would meet at home after work, prepare supper together, and then go for walks in the nearby park.

It wasn't long before children were born, and Chad and Maria enjoyed working together at parenting as well. Maria lived with a daily sense of blessing; with a loving husband and three beautiful children, what more could she want? Then in an instant it all changed.

She knew something was wrong when Chad showed up at the house at 2:00 p.m. on a Tuesday. He was seldom ever home before 6:00 p.m. Chad didn't have to say anything; Maria knew something terrible had happened by the look on his face. "Maria, I've lost my job and right now I don't want to talk about it," Chad said angrily and went upstairs to the den.

Over the next few days Maria was able to pry the story out of Chad. Changes in the industry had caused Chad's firm to shut down his entire department. Not only had he lost his job, but in the region where he and Maria lived there wouldn't be any work in his field for the foreseeable future. He was left with a three-month severance and little hope of finding work at the same income level.

As the weeks slipped by, Maria began to realize that Chad's shock and anger weren't going away. Her once-relational husband had become a sullen man. Chad quit helping with supper and had no interest in the family walks. He had little to say to his wife and children, and the computer in the den became his closest friend.

Maria tried to be sympathetic and understanding at first. She would leave little notes and cards of encouragement. She would surprise Chad with one of his favorite meals. She would plan things for them to do together, things she knew Chad would enjoy. But Chad walked around like a man who hated his life, and nothing seemed to pull him out of it.

Maria began to tire of walking on eggshells, of going places by herself, of having one event after another ruined by Chad's anger. She grew tired of making excuses for her husband and couldn't believe what her life had become. She was increasingly envious of wives in other marriages. She dreaded waking up each morning to the fact that Chad was still in bed and wouldn't be getting up anytime soon.

After a few months, Chad found a job in a different industry. It offered him little satisfaction and he had to start at the bottom of the ladder. Finances were tough so the family moved into a smaller home in a less affluent neighborhood. It was settling in on Maria that recovery, if it came at all, was going to be a long, slow road. She had exhausted all her efforts to cajole, nag, threaten, seduce, or bargain Chad into change. Somehow the corrupting essence of the awful afternoon he lost his job had spread over everything. Chad went to work begrudgingly and came home to spend hours on YouTube every night. He had little to do with his family and had long since quit going to church. From Maria's perspective, Chad had simply stopped being Chad.

Maria was hurt, angry, and helpless. She felt robbed. It seemed like someone had kidnapped her real husband and returned to her this defective clone. She couldn't understand how a God of love would allow such a thing to happen, and it didn't feel at all like God was helping her to make it through. Maria quit going to her small group. It was full of couples and the whole experience had just become too painful and embarrassing. She didn't abandon the Lord, and she still prayed, but God seemed distant and the joy of her faith was long gone.

Maria was being called to the hardest thing she had ever faced. She was being called to wait. She was being called to acknowledge how little control she had over her own circumstances and that she was not the center of her own universe. Maria was being called to submit to the choices of the One who is truly in control of her world. She was being called to do what is right in the face of what is wrong. She was being called to wait, and she was finding it to be the most difficult discipline she had ever encountered.

What Is Waiting?

It may seem like a dumb question, but I do think a definition of waiting will be helpful. In the sense I mean, waiting is living through those moments when you *do not understand* what God is doing and you *have no power* to change your circumstances for the better.

The definition tells you why this kind of waiting is hard—because it takes you beyond the bounds of your own wisdom, understanding, and ability. So much of our daily comfort comes from the fact that we are able to make sense of our circumstances. Sensible things usually aren't so difficult to deal with. Being able to wrap our minds around a situation makes us feel as if we can control it, or at least that control is possible. We don't tend to get as anxious about things that we think can be understood and altered.

We all want life to make sense, and we want it to yield to our efforts to improve it. These desires are not bad in themselves, but the struggle comes when these desires are not met, forcing us to wait. The struggle is really what this is all about. To understand your struggle with waiting, you must begin here: waiting will always reveal the true character of your heart.

Sometimes, the trial of waiting exposes a lack of *saving* faith in someone who was behaving culturally as a Christian but had not come to trust God for salvation. But among those who truly have been saved, waiting in the face of challenging circumstances exposes our *level* of faith, our capacity to truly leave things up to God, our ability to rest in God and God alone.

Theoretical faith is always easier than practical, functional faith, and when we are faced with the challenge of waiting it can be disturbing to realize how little of that real-life faith we have. When forced to wait, we may find that what has given us peace and rest is not a solid, functional confidence in God's presence, promises, power, wisdom, and love. Perhaps instead what has given us our inner sense of well-being is our ability to figure life out and our seeming power to control our circumstances, whether through intelligence, determination, prosperity, or something else. When God calls us to wait through circumstances we cannot understand and in places where important things are out of our control, losing that inner peace can make life unbearably difficult.

Waiting will always reveal where you have placed your hope. Your heart is always exposed by the *way* that you wait.

If your hope is in your power, you will find it extremely difficult to live through situations where you have been revealed to be powerless. If your hope is in your wisdom, you will find it extremely difficult to deal with circumstances that simply make no sense to you. If your hope has been in a certain person or situation, you will find it very hard to deal with it should that person or situation radically change. Think about it. If my hope and confidence were really in the wisdom and power of the Lord, I would not find this kind of waiting so hard. Waiting is hard precisely because it calls us to live by faith and not by sight. That was Maria's struggle. It is the struggle of us all.

Why Are We Called to Wait?

There are lots of good reasons why waiting is not merely inescapable, but necessary and helpful. Here are some of those reasons.

Because We Live in a Fallen World

We are called to wait because the broken-down-house condition of the world makes everything we do harder. Nothing in this life really functions as originally intended. Something changed when sin entered the world, and in rebuking Adam, God summarized that change: "cursed is the ground . . . through painful toil you will eat of it . . . It will produce thorns and thistles for you . . . By the sweat of your brow you will eat your food" (Genesis 3:17–19). Sin brought friction and trouble and pain and sweat and a thousand other "thorn and thistle" complications to absolutely every aspect of life. We find ourselves waiting because everything in a fallen world is more laborious and entangled than it really ought to be.

Sin also put greed and fear and arrogance and jealousy and self-worship into the souls of all who live this thorn-and-thistle life. We must wait because, by being selfish, impatient, competitive, driven, anxious, and angry, we make life harder for one another in an endless variety of ways. This is why the seemingly easy conversation becomes the full-blown conflict, why the once-sweet relationship gets stained with hurt and acrimony, and why government often functions as a tool of personal power rather than an instrument of community protection and service.

Processes and people are all affected—everything and everyone has been damaged by the Fall. We must wait, because in a world that is broken everything we do is harder and more complicated than it was ever meant to be.

Because God Is Sovereign

We must wait because we are not writing our own stories. Life does not work the way we want it to, in the time we want it to. You and I do not live in the center of the universe. That place is forever occupied by God and God alone. Our individual stories are part of the great origin-to-destiny story that he alone authors. Waiting becomes immediately easier when you realize God is sovereign (and you are not) and when you further reflect on the reality that he is the ultimate source of everything that is wise, loving, and good.

Waiting, therefore, is not a sign that your world is out of control. Rather, it is a sign that your world is under the wise and infinitely attentive control of a God of fathomless wisdom and boundless love. This means you can rest as you wait, not because you like to wait, but because you trust the One who is calling you to wait.

Because God Is a God of Grace

Waiting is one of God's most powerful tools of grace. God doesn't just give us grace *for* the wait. The wait *itself* is a gift of grace. You see, waiting is not only about what you will receive at the end of the wait. Waiting is about what you will become *as* you wait.

In calling us to wait, God is rescuing us from our bondage to our own plan, our own wisdom, our own power, our own control. In calling us to wait, God is freeing us from the claustrophobic confines of our own little kingdoms of one and drawing us into a greater allegiance to his Kingdom of glory and grace. Waiting is more than being patient as situations and *other* people change. Waiting is about understanding that you and I desperately need to change, and that waiting is a powerful tool of personal change. God is using the grace of waiting to change us at the causal core of our personhood, the heart. Now that's a good thing!

So We Can Minister to Others

Waiting is central to any ministry activity. If you are truly committed to being part of what God is doing in the lives of others, you will be willing to wait. Personal heart and life change is seldom a sudden event. Usually it is a process. You and I do not determine when and how the winds of the Spirit will blow, and people do not often become what they need to become overnight.

This means that in ministry we are called to have the same conversation again and again. We are called to pick that person up after each failure, to be willing to forgive and forbear, to remind him or her once more of God's presence and grace, and to be willing to have our lives slowed down and complicated in the process. People of grace and love are always people who are willing to wait.

For the Increase of God's Glory

Finally, we are called to wait because everything that exists, exists not for our comfort and ease but for God's glory. The whole redemptive story is written for one purpose and one purpose alone, the glory of the King.

Waiting is hard for us because we tie our hearts to other glories. We so often live for the glory of human acceptance, of personal achievement, of power and position, of possessions and places, and of comfort and pleasure. So when God's glory requires that these things be withheld from us—things we look to for identity, meaning, and purpose—we find waiting a grueling, burdensome experience.

Waiting means surrendering your glory. Waiting means submitting to his glory. Waiting means understanding that you were given life and breath for the glory of another. Waiting gives you opportunity to forsake the delusion of your own glory and rest in the God of awesome glory. Only when you do that will you find what you seek, and what you were meant to have: lasting identity, meaning, purpose, and peace in Christ.

How to Wait Productively

So what does it look like to wait in a way that makes you a participant in what God is doing rather than someone who struggles against the wait? Let me suggest several things.

Remind Yourself You Are Not Alone in the Wait

As you wait, tell yourself again and again that you have not been singled out. Remind yourself that you are part of a vast company of people who are being called to wait. Reflect on the biblical story. Abraham waited many years for his promised son. Israel waited 420 years for deliverance from Egypt, then another 40 years before they could enter the land God had promised them. God's people waited generation after generation for the Messiah, and the church now waits for his return. The whole world groans as it waits for the final renewal of all things that God has promised. You see, waiting is not an interruption of God's plan. It *is* his plan. And you can know this as well: the Lord who has called you to wait is with you in your wait. He hasn't gone off to do something else, like the doctor whose appointment you wait for. No, God is near and he provides for you all that you need to be able to wait.

Realize That Waiting Is Active

I think that usually our view of waiting *is* the doctor's office. We see it as a meaningless waste of time, like a man stuck in the reception area until he has nothing left to do but scan recipes in a two-year-old copy of *Ladies' Home Journal*.

Our waiting on God must not be understood this way. The sort of waiting to which we are called as Christians is not inactivity. It is very positive, purposeful, and spiritual. To be called to wait is to be called to the activity of remembering: remembering who I am and who God is. To be called to wait is to be called to the activity of worship: worshiping God for his presence, wisdom, power, love, and grace. To be called to wait is to be called to the activity of serving: looking for ways to lovingly assist and encourage others who are also being called to wait. To be called to wait is to be called to the activity of praying; confessing the struggles of my heart and seeking the grace of the God who has called me to wait. We must rethink waiting, and remind ourselves that waiting is itself a call to action.

Celebrate How Little Control You Have

Because the constant striving to be a little god over some corner of creation is draining and futile, waiting should actually be a relief. It's a reminder that I don't have as much power and control as I thought I had. When I am required to wait I realize again that I do not have to load the world onto my shoulders. I may have God-given responsibilities in a number of areas, but that is vastly different from pretending I have sovereignty in any area. The world is being carried on the capable shoulders of the King of Kings. All I am responsible for is the job description of character and behavior that this King has called me to in his Word. The remainder I am free to entrust to him, and for that I am very, very thankful! He really does have the whole world in his hands.

Celebrate God's Commitment to His Work of Grace

As you are waiting, reflect on how deeply broken the world that you live in actually is. Reflect on how pervasive your own struggle with sin really is. Then celebrate the fact that God is committed to the countless ways, large and small, in which his grace is at work to accomplish his purposes.

When it comes to the ongoing work of grace, he is a dissatisfied Redeemer. He will not forsake the work of his hands until all has been fully restored. He will exercise his power in whatever way is necessary so that we can finally be fully redeemed from this broken world and delivered from the sin that has held us fast. Celebrate the fact that God will not forsake that process of grace in your life in order to deliver to you the momentary comfort, pleasure, and ease that you would rather have in your time of exhaustion, discouragement, and weakness. He simply loves you too much to exchange temporary gratification for eternal glory!

Let Your Waiting Strengthen Your Faith

As I think about waiting, I often remember what is said of Abraham in Romans 4:18–21. The passage tells us that as he waited, Abraham was strengthened in his faith. Now, that's not what we would expect, is it? We tend to think that, having been given a promise from God, a person might well *begin* to wait with vibrant faith, but as the wait drags on it seems like that faith would gradually weaken. So, why did Abraham's faith on the whole grow stronger and stronger? Because of what he did as he waited. During his wait, Abraham became a student of the character and power of God, and the more he saw God for who he is, the stronger his faith became.

There are three ways in which, like Abraham, you can let your waiting strengthen your faith. You can recognize that waiting is an opportunity to know *God* better through spending time in his Word, thus developing a deeper sense of his character, wisdom, power, and plan. Second, you can recognize that waiting is an opportunity to know *yourself* better. As you wait, and as your heart is revealed, you have the precious opportunity to become a student of your own heart. What sins, weaknesses, and struggles has God revealed during the wait? Where has waiting exposed the lies and false gods that make waiting difficult? And third, you can recognize that waiting is an opportunity to know *others* better, as their hearts are similarly revealed. This can offer you precious opportunities for effective ministry.

Determine to grow stronger, more effective, and more full of faith as you wait. It is, after all, a key part of God's intention.

Count Your Blessings

Vital to productive waiting is a commitment to resist the grumbling and complaining that often kidnap us all. To fight this tendency, learn to number your blessings as you wait.

I once heard a missionary leader tell a story of how he was dreading an extremely long road trip. Then the thought came to him that this time of being imprisoned behind the wheel of his car was in fact an opportunity. He decided that as he drove he would thank God for every little detail of blessing and grace he could recall, beginning with his earliest memory. As he drove hour after hour, he recounted to God year after year and decade after decade of blessing upon blessing. By the end of his journey, he still had not come up to the present day. As a result, rather than ending his trip exhausted and bored, he ended it excited and changed. He saw his life through new eyes, with the presence and provision of God in his life taking on a clarity and comprehensiveness he had never before glimpsed.

By contrast, waiting often becomes for us an exercise in reminding ourselves of what we don't have. How much better, how much more fruitful, how much more joyful, to take waiting as an opportunity to recount the many, many good things in our lives that we have been given—things we could have never earned, achieved, or deserved.

Long for Eternity

There is one other thing waiting is meant to do. God intends that waiting would make me long for home. When I consider this, I am often reminded of camping. I suspect the whole purpose of camping is to make you thankful for home. When you camp, everything is more difficult than it would be at home. In the beginning, that can be fun. But three or four days in, you begin to get tired of having to make a fire, having to hunt for drinkable water, and having to fish for supper. You quietly (or not so quietly) begin to long for home.

Waiting is meant to remind you that you live "between the already and the not yet." Yes, there are many, many things for which to be thankful in this life, but this place is not your final home. You are in a temporary dwelling in a temporary location. In everything you experience here, there is one aspect or another that can remind you this is not home. The hardships of your present world speak clearly: this is not the final destination. Waiting is meant to produce in you a God-honoring dissatisfaction with the status quo. Waiting is meant to make you hungry, to produce in you a longing. For what? To be home—home with your Lord forever, home where sin is no more, home in a world that has been made completely new. As you wait, keep telling yourself, "This is not my final destination."

Right now, right here, there is some way, perhaps many ways, in which God is calling you to wait. How well are you waiting?

Has your waiting produced in you a faith that is stronger? Or weaker? Has the manner of your waiting drawn you closer to God? Or further away? Has your approach to waiting helped remind you of all the blessings you have been showered with? Or has it tempted you to continually rehearse your list of unmet wants? Has your waiting served to teach you truths about yourself? Or has it only made you more blind about yourself and angry about your circumstances? Has the way you wait enabled you to reach out and minister to others better, or has it simply drawn you deeper into the claustrophobic drama of your own waiting?

In each case, it's your choice. Take hold of the grace that God makes available. All of these outcomes are contingent on whether you choose God or self, fruitfulness or futility, his powerful grace or your own feeble will. Always remember that God is never separate from your wait. He is the Lord of waiting. Because your wait is not outside of his plan, but a vital and necessary part of it, he is with you in your wait. As you wait, tell yourself again and again: *Waiting is not just about what I get at the end of the wait, but about who I become as I wait.*

Good and Angry

It's an everyday
experience,
a bit of a source of
embarrassment.
It is more of a theme
than I would care to
admit.
It's revealed in moments of
low-grade irritation
grumbling impatience
quickly-expressed complaints
argumentative responses
looks of dissatisfaction.
I am angry,
no, not because
my world is broken,
no, not because
injustice exists,
no, not because
prejudice still lives,
no, not because
war and violence
destroy lives and
communities,
no, not because
falsehood gets a wider hearing
than truth,
no, not because
of the suffering that is all
around me.

No,
I am angry because
I want to be in control.
I am angry because
people and things get in my
way.
So, I cry out for Your
help.
I seek your
rescue,
not that I would be anger free,
but that I would be
good and angry
at the same time.

10

Be Good and Angry

*L*et me introduce you to two angry men, starting with Tom. Tom has been angry for a long time. Anger is the theme that runs through each of his days, the forge that shapes the situations and relationships of his life. Tom's wife and kids are used to his anger. They stay out of his way in the morning because Tom greets the day like a man possessed. He allows nothing to alter his morning routine. The bathroom had better be empty when Tom needs it, and his coffee and toast had better be ready when he wants them. After all, there are only a certain number of minutes in the day, with many tasks to complete, and this leaves no time for unexpected "hassles."

Tom's kids have learned not to talk with Tom in the morning about money needs, or school problems, or really much of anything. They have learned the hard way not to argue in Dad's hearing. They have also learned that when he says it's time for family worship (the last thing that happens before Tom leaves for work), they had better drop whatever they are doing and come quickly.

Tom does a lot of talking to the traffic as he negotiates through near-gridlock conditions on his way to work. Before he hits the parking lot he is already complaining to himself about what his day will be like, about all those workers who "don't have a shred of a clue what they are doing." Tom's the boss, but he doesn't feel like the boss. He feels like a man under siege. He feels like few people listen to him and no one really respects his authority. Sure, Tom can be friendly, and he doesn't lead like an autocrat. But when things go wrong, his anger comes quickly.

It's not unusual for Tom to return home at the end of the day a bit disgusted. Not with his home life, but simply because he has carried the problems of the day into the house with him. His kids have learned to pick up on their father's mood before they come too close. They know he will immediately look for the paper, which had better be there, and then ask how long until supper, which had better be soon.

Yes, Tom is a hard worker and a good provider. And yes, with his business and four children he has a lot on his plate. And no, Tom isn't abusive or violent. But Tom is a very angry man and that anger stains everything he touches.

Jim is angry too, really angry, but his is not an anger that makes his family walk on eggshells. Jim's anger doesn't make him grumble his way to work. It doesn't make him look down on the people who work for him. It doesn't shape the way he enters the house at the end of his work day. Yet Jim is certainly an angry man.

Jim is angry that years of political corruption have left the city, which he lives in and loves, a shell of what it once was. Jim is angry at the poverty and violence that makes neighborhoods not too far from him dangerous and unlivable. Jim is angry that art and culture have been so infected with sex and violence that it is almost impossible to be entertained without having your morals assaulted. Jim is angry that he cannot send his children to the schools his taxes pay for because those schools are so broken that little in the way of good education actually takes place there.

Jim is angry that the church has been either so isolated from the surrounding culture, or in such a war with it, that it has lost its ability to be the salt and light God intends it to be. Jim is angry at the materialism and passivity that keep him and his fellow believers from doing the transformative things that only believers could ever do.

But Jim's is not an anger that craves more control. He doesn't pray that things will go his way. Jim usually prays that somehow, some way, he would be part of what God is doing in the place where he has been sent. You see, Jim's anger isn't about Jim at all. It isn't formed out of the plans and purposes of a claustrophobic kingdom of one. Instead, Jim is a man who knows what it means to be good and angry at the very same time. Jim's anger is the righteous anger of a man who loves God and whose heart has been caught up in the purposes of God's kingdom. Jim's anger isn't the anger of demanding tones and ugly words. It isn't the "I'm in charge here" anger of impatience and quick irritation. It isn't the anger that causes complaints to come quickly and dissatisfaction to be a daily theme.

Jim is angry, very angry, at what sin has done to the world where he lives. This makes his anger full of compassion, wisdom, justice, kindness, and love. Jim anger's relieves the distress of others, rather than adding to it. Jim's anger doesn't allow him to be self-focused. No, it calls him to be involved in the suffering of others and to look for ways to bless them with what is good. Jim's anger doesn't allow him to be selfish with his time or tight with his money. Jim's anger causes him to find joy in investing himself and his resources in the Kingdom that has won his heart.

Tom and Jim are two angry men whose lives are radically different, and whose angers produce radically different results. Tom is angry because he wants to be God, so he has reduced everything in his life down to the size of his little kingdom of one. His anger is leaving a legacy of fear, hurt, and separation. But Jim's anger honors God by putting God and his Kingdom in their rightful place. Jim's anger is leaving a legacy of love, compassion, provision, and healing.

There is probably never a day when you aren't angry in some way. Are you good and angry at the same time? How much of your anger has anything at all to do with the Kingdom of God?

Anger Is Essential

In a world that has been terribly broken by sin, in a world where nothing operates as was intended, and in a world where evil often has more immediate influence than good, it would be wrong not to be angry. How can you look poverty in the face and not be angry? How can you consider the surge of AIDS and not be angry? How could you look at the political corruption that makes government more a place for personal power than societal protection, and not be angry? How can you look at the rate of divorce in Western culture, or the prevalence of domestic violence, and not be angry? How can you consider the huge numbers of homeless people who wander our streets and not be angry? How can you consider the confusion of gender identity and sexual impropriety that is everywhere around us and not be angry? How can you consider the state of our educational institutions, the state of art and culture, and the state of popular entertainment and not be angry? How can you look at the state of the church, which seems so often to have lost its way, and not be angry? How can you even look at your own life, your own family, and your own circle of friends—how sin twists and complicates every location, relationship, and situation of your life—and not be angry?

How can you consider disease, war, and environmental distress and not be angry? How can you look at the fact that nothing in your world is exactly as it was meant to be and not be angry? You simply cannot look at the world with the eyes of truth and with a heart committed to what God says is right and good, and not be angry at the state of things in this fallen world. In a fallen world, anger is a good thing. In a fallen world, anger is a constructive thing. In a fallen world, anger is an essential thing.

That is, if the anger is about something bigger than you.

In a fallen world, people of character and conscience will always be angry. Perhaps our problem regarding anger is not just that we are often angry for the wrong reasons, but that we are not angry often enough for the right reasons. Perhaps our problem is that the things that should make us angry and thereby move us to action just don't make us angry anymore.

So we get used to political corruption. We get used to homelessness. We get used to the perverse morals of the entertainment industry. We get used to how many broken families are around us. We get used to the daily reports of suffering and disease that infect every continent on the globe. We get used to the fact that the church is often a place of compromise and division. We get used to our own complacency and hypocrisy. We get used to marital stresses and childhood rebellion. We get used to a world that has been broken by sin.

We learn to walk around the problems, almost as if they aren't there. We learn the skill of negotiating the minefields. The fact that life is broken becomes a regular part of our lives and simply doesn't bother us any longer. We develop the sad capacity not to care anymore about things that should break our hearts and rile us up. We lose our moral edge and don't even realize it. Things that God says are not okay become okay to us. We lose our ability, our commitment, to be good and angry at the same time.

You see, righteous anger is not optional. For people who have accepted God's calling on their lives, for people who claim to be living for something bigger than their own happiness, and for people who profess to be committed to what is right, true, loving, and good, such anger is a calling. You cannot be like God and be free of anger as long as you live in a sin-broken world.

What If God Wasn't Angry?
We all need to reevaluate how we think about the anger of God. Sometimes we can treat God's anger like we treat the embarrassing uncle in our extended family. We work hard to keep this attribute of God away from public exposure. Are we worried about causing undue embarrassment to the family of faith? We act as if anger were the dark side of God's character that we need to keep hidden.

God doesn't have a dark side! John says, "God is light; in him there is no darkness at all" (1 John 1:5). It is impossible for there to be anything evil in God. It is impossible for him to feel or act unrighteously. He is entirely holy in every respect. He is completely good in everything he does. He is not evil, cannot be tempted by evil, and does not tempt anyone to do evil. He is perfectly holy, always, and in every possible way.

Now, all of this has very important implications for us as we seek to live productively in this fallen world. The primary implication is that if God is holy and angry at the same time, then anger is not evil in and of itself. If it were, God would never be angry. The many passages which teach us that God *is* angry simply would not be in the Bible (see Exodus 32:10, 34:6; Deuteronomy 29:28; 2 Kings 22:13; Psalms 2:12, 30:5; Romans 1:18; and more). Therefore, it is not merely *possible* to be holy and angry at the same time, it is a *calling*. The Christian who actively recognizes and treasures the unchanging holiness of God will find it impossible to be in contact with anything that is in any way evil and *not* be angry.

This means that if we are to take seriously our call to imitate our Father in heaven, to act and respond as he does within our human limitations, and thereby to be part of what he is doing on earth, one of the things we must be is *angry*. Not angry like Tom. Not angry because we are not getting our own way. But angry like Jim. Angry in the face of anything that is a violation of what God says is right, good, loving, and true.

The Anger of Grace

Let's be very clear here. God's anger is the anger of grace. It is not the violent anger of unbridled fury. God's anger always works to right what is wrong. That is what grace does. This gracious anger has two sides to it: justice and mercy.

In the gracious anger of justice, God works to punish wrong, but he does even more. God is not satisfied merely with punishing wrong. His hunger for right is so strong that he will not relent until wrong has been completely destroyed. He will not rest until evil is no more and justice and righteousness reign forever and ever!

There is also another side to his gracious anger. It is the anger of mercy. In mercy he works to *convict*, that is, to produce in us a sorrow for the wrongs that we think, say, and do. In mercy he works to *forgive*, that is, to clear our moral debt. In mercy he works to *empower*, that is, to give us everything we need to resist wrong and to do what is right. And in mercy he works to *deliver*. As I said earlier, he is a dissatisfied Redeemer, who will not be satisfied until every microbe of sin is completely eradicated from every cell of the heart of every one of his children.

Where do we see both sides of God's anger coming together in one moment? On that hill outside the city gates where Jesus hung. That is where we see justice and mercy kiss. As he hung there, Jesus bore the full weight of the *justice* of God's anger. He paid the penalty our sin required. And on the cross Jesus became the instrument of the *mercy* of God's anger that every sinner needs. He purchased our forgiveness.

If God were incapable of anger, there would have been no cross. Without the cross, there would be no hope of the final victory of righteousness, mercy, and justice. We would be living in a world where evil exists inside of us and outside of us and there would be nothing that we could do about it. The entire world and everyone in it would literally be going to hell and we would be along for the ride with no way of getting off. We would be both the victims and victimizers living in a now and future hell of separation from God and everything that is good, watching darkness get darker with no hope of light.

You see, anger is one of God's most beautiful characteristics. For God's children, his anger is a place of bright hope. Because he is righteously angry with sin every day, we can rest assured that everything sin has broken will be restored. Everything sin has twisted will be straightened. Everything that has gone wrong will be made right again. God's anger assures us that all things will be made new.

Anger Is a Calling

The prophet Micah writes, "He has showed you, O man, what is good. And what does the Lord require of you? To act justly and to love mercy and to walk humbly with your God" (Micah 6:8). This passage is a call to righteous anger. It is a call to be an instrument of the gracious anger of God. What will cause you to act justly? Is it not righteous indignation at the perversion of justice that causes innocent people to suffer and permits the guilty to go free? What will cause you to respond to others in mercy? Is it not your anger at the suffering that is all around you in this broken world? If you want to be part of what God is doing, will you not hate what he hates?

Suffering must not, cannot be okay with us. Injustice must not, cannot be okay with us. The immorality of the culture around us must not, cannot be okay with us. The deceit of the atheistic worldview—the philosophical paradigm of many of our institutions—must not, cannot be okay with us. Righteous anger should yank all of us out of selfish passivity. Righteous anger should call all of us to be part of God's revolution of grace. It should propel all of us to do anything we can to lift the load of people's suffering and to bring them into the freedom of God's truth.

What is this anger like? It is kind and compassionate. It is tender and giving. It is patient and perseverant. It will make your heart open and your conscience sensitive. It will cause you to slow down and pay attention. It will cause you to expand the borders of your concern beyond you and yours. It will cost you money, time, energy, and strength. It will fill up your schedule and complicate your life. It will mean sacrifice and suffering. When you're both good and angry, you won't be content with establishing your own comfort and ease. When you're both good and angry, you won't fill your life so full with meeting your own needs that you have little time for meeting the needs of others.

But all of this requires war. Not war with people or institutions. No, this is an internal war. It is a war of the heart. Sin turns us in on ourselves. It makes us demanding, critical, cold, and self-focused. Sin is self-absorbed and anti-social. So kindness, compassion, gentleness, mercy, love, patience, and grace sadly do not come naturally to any of us. They only come when grace wins the war for our hearts. This is a war between God's will and our will, between God's plan and our plan, between God's desire and our desire, and between God's sovereignty and our quest for self-rule. It is a war fought in every situation and location of our lives.

At the level of our hearts, the reason we don't reach out to assist those in need is because we simply don't care. We sadly have the capacity to look at the dilemmas of others and not be moved. Rather than act to serve others in the realities of their struggles, we try to co-opt others into serving us in our little kingdoms of personal pleasure and self-love. Does this all seem too negative and harsh to you? I would ask you again, how much of the anger of your last few weeks had anything whatsoever to do with the Kingdom of God. Convicting, isn't it?

So, if we are ever going to be tools of the gracious anger of a righteous and loving God, we must begin by admitting to the coldness and selfishness of our own hearts. We must cry out for the rescue that only his grace can give. We must pray for eyes that can see and hearts that are willing. We must make strategic decisions to put ourselves where need exists. We must determine to slow down so that when opportunities for mercy present themselves we are not too distracted or too busy.

Most of all, we need to pray that we would be angry. We must pray that a holy zeal for what is right and good would so fill our hearts that the evils around us, that greet us daily, would not be okay with us. We must pray that we would be angry until there is no reason to be angry anymore. And we must be vigilant, looking for every opportunity to express the righteous indignation of justice, mercy, wisdom, grace, compassion, patience, perseverance, and love. We must be agitated and restless until his kingdom has finally come and his will is finally being done on earth as it is in heaven. For the sake of his honor and his kingdom, we must determine to be good and angry at the same time.

This week you will be angry. Everyone is in some way. What will the legacy of this week's anger be for you? Will it help build a legacy like Tom's, or like Jim's? Will your anger propel you to be a healer, a restorer, a rescuer, and a reconciler? Or will your anger leave a legacy of fear, hurt, disappointment, and division?

God calls you to be good and he calls you to be angry. This broken world desperately needs people who will answer his call.

PART TWO

Doing

The Good Life

Easy to be
passive
Easy to avoid
involvement
Easy to
look the other way
Easy to shut up
your heart
Easy to focus on
me and mine
Easy to withhold
compassion
Easy to
shut the door and close the blinds
Easy to love
what is lovely
Easy to give to
what will bring a return
Easy to build a fence around
your comfort
too high to see over
with no gate for exit.
Easy to sit in the middle
and call it the good life.

11

Reject Passivity

They were three sixteen-year-old boys. They had little in the way of power and authority. No one expected much of them; just to go to class and do their homework. They were just three teenage boys. Every adult around them would have been thankful if they had simply avoided the normal teenage temptations and errors.

None of them was a student leader. None of them looked like the kid who would make a difference. They were just three teenage boys. But they were about to forever change their surroundings because they refused to be passive in the face of wrong.

The boys were attending a large and well-known Christian school that had been around for years. But there were problems in the school like never before. The student body had become divided, with a separation between the "suburban" kids and the "city" kids. But really, those labels were just a cover. This once-great school had become racially divided in a very obvious way. The tensions between the black kids and the white kids only seemed to grow each week. There hadn't been any violence, at least not yet. And much of the racism was covert. But it was there, and real, and undeniable.

This was not acceptable to the boys. Theirs was a *Christian* school. It was supposed to be known for its love. It was supposed to be a place of peace. It proclaimed a message that all people are equally needy in God's eyes. Yet the culture of this school had become defined by worldly stereotypes and division, nothing at all like the rapprochement and unity that ought to have prevailed. They were just three teenage boys, but after many conversations about the culture of their school, they decided to do something.

There in his office, having a conversation he never could have imagined that day, the headmaster found their idea a little scary, but the boys were politely not taking no for an answer. He realized it could all go wrong, yet the zeal of the three was compelling. Plus, they were right: the racism was real and growing worse. So he allowed them to try holding a weekly Friday-afternoon discussion on race relations in the school. He directed them to get two teachers to give oversight to the gatherings, which the boys did. And, as they had asked, he arranged for information to be included in each Friday's morning announcements, broadcast to the homerooms.

That first Friday, a racially mixed group of twenty-five uncomfortable teenagers gathered in the assigned classroom, with the three original boys the only ones actually looking like they wanted to be there. But something began to happen that day. One of the three boys started the conversation by confessing his own hurt and bias. Voice after voice followed. Sometimes it was confession, sometimes confrontation, but honesty ruled that hour. No, nothing had changed, but a door had been opened that would be hard to close.

The following week, fifty high-schoolers piled into that classroom and the conversation began to migrate from confession and confrontation to reconciliation. There were even times when students would get up, walk across the room, and embrace one another in a public gesture of respect. The third week, the gathering had to be held in the auditorium. It had become positively uncool not to be there. The three boys had learned how to make the gatherings productive and they led them well.

These three are not teenagers anymore. They have grown up and moved on, but their legacy remains. That school is more racially unified than it would have ever been otherwise, and it is only because three mostly unremarkable teenage boys would not remain passive. They rejected the unbiblical status quo they experienced every day, and refused to be quiet about it. Just three regular teenage boys, but they left something beautiful behind.

You Have Every Reason to Be Passive

One way our particular "house" gets even more broken down is when we neglect preventive maintenance. As we look around and take an honest inventory, we can become overwhelmed with all the individual repairs that would be needed to restore the place to its original glory. Apart from an active faith in God's sovereignty and grace, it's easy to throw up our hands and adopt a "What's the use?" mentality. If it's going to be so hard to make really significant improvements, what does it matter if things deteriorate a little further?

This sort of faithless attitude could apply to the "house" that is our life, or the "house" that is the regular environment in which we live and work—such as the school attended by those young men. We could all come up with lots of good reasons to remain passive. The problems seem too numerous, and many seem too large. You see yourself as one little person, in one little place, at one little moment in time, and it just doesn't seem logical that you could make any difference at all. To be specific, let me propose three arguments that we all tend to make at one time or another that keep us passive and uninvolved.

The Identity Argument: "I'm Too Small"

As we have already discussed in this book, you and I don't have much in the way of personal power and authority. When we think about it, we know we can't really change people, and we know that in most important respects we have little ability to alter circumstances significantly. When we compare ourselves to the size of the changes that are needed around our "house," it is easy to conclude that God must actually be mistaken on this whole subject of renovation.

Remember the first words from Moses' mouth when God called him to go back to Egypt and lead out the Israelites? Moses said, "Who am I, that I should go to Pharaoh and bring the Israelites out of Egypt?" (Exodus 3:11). In response, God restates Moses' commission, and Moses basically replies, "But I'm not sure I know what to say." So God tells him what to say, tells him that he will go with him, and tells him that he will accompany Moses' words with "wonders" that will strike the Egyptians. Moses tries once again to take himself out of the action, essentially replying, "But what if they do not believe me?"

So the Lord, right there and then, demonstrates two miraculous signs that he will allow Moses to perform before Pharaoh. But these still aren't enough for Moses, so he says, "O, Lord, I have never been eloquent, neither in the past nor since you have spoken to your servant. I am slow of speech and tongue" (Exodus 4:10). Through a series of questions God then reminds Moses that he made his mouth. But Moses is still not convinced that he can do what God is calling him to do and finally pleads, "Oh, my Lord, please send someone else." The Bible says that at that point the anger of the Lord burned against Moses, that God gave Aaron to Moses as his spokesman, and that God sent Moses to do what he had chosen him to do.

There are two ways to look at how Moses responded here, and both are true. In one sense, Moses was accurately identifying weaknesses in himself. Fair enough, but hardly the complete picture because, far more importantly, Moses was completely overlooking the fact that the one asking him to do these significant things was the Almighty Creator, who certainly had the power to bring them to pass.

So the kind of doubt Moses was displaying here was not simply doubt in his own abilities. There is ultimately a deeper and far more significant doubt involved—a doubt of God's sovereignty and power. Where the first kind of doubt might be a form of humility, the second is a sinful faithlessness. God *knows* that in ourselves we are not up to the tasks he calls us to, but he never makes a false assignment. When he sends us we are sent as instruments in his almighty hands. He is the one who creates the change. He is the great Restorer. He never calls us to what we cannot accomplish in him, but he always calls us to what we could never accomplish without him.

God did eventually do amazing things through weak and fearful Moses. Pharaoh was silenced, Egypt was defeated, and the children of Israel were liberated. You see, for the child of God, passivity is simply rooted in poor theology. When you begin to embrace the theology of God's presence, promises, and power, passivity no longer makes any sense.

The Magnitude Argument: "The Problem Is Too Big"

Maybe you're looking at the chaotic life of a loved one and are overwhelmed at all that needs to change. Or maybe you're considering your marriage, and all the years that have poured over the dam, and it simply seems impossible to turn it around. Or maybe in studying your community you're stunned at the injustice, corruption, poverty, and violence not too far from you—conditions that seem far too big, far too complicated, and goodness, it's all been going on for years.

141

Once more, Moses comes to mind. The children of Israel are now in the wilderness and complaining because they are bored with eating the manna that God provides every day to sustain them. God tells Moses that he will send quail for Israel to eat; not just for a meal, or a week's meals, but for a month, until it comes out of their noses and they loathe it! (Numbers 11:18–20). Now read Moses' words, and you can then understand what is wrong with the magnitude argument.

> But Moses said, "Here I am among six hundred thousand men on foot, and you say, 'I will give them meat to eat for a whole month!' Would they have enough if flocks and herds were slaughtered for them? Would they have enough if all the fish in the sea were caught for them?"
>
> —Numbers 11:21–22

What do you think is wrong with Moses' analysis? He certainly recognizes, legitimately, that it will take a great deal of food to feed more than 600,000 hungry Israelites. But he can't see past that fact. The fatal flaw in his analysis is that he thinks far too little of the God who is calling him to act. We know this from God's answer. "Is the LORD's arm too short? You will now see whether or not what I say will come true for you" (Numbers 11:23). In Moses' eyes, the God whom he serves is infinitely smaller than the God who actually exists and who has called him to do great things. No problem is too big for the Creator God.

The Separation Argument: "It's Not My Problem"

One way we sometimes try to quiet a guilty conscience is to tell ourselves that we would gladly *get* involved if we *were* involved. We argue that we have a lot on our plate already and we want to be faithful to what God has given us to do. Again, there is some logic to this, and even some truth. You are a human being with limited time, energy, and resources. And it is true that you must make a priority of the things God has given you to do. But perhaps we take ourselves off the hook too easily. Perhaps we are often too happily uninvolved.

Could it be that our passivity to the needs around us does not really grow out of a commitment to prioritize what God has commanded us to *do*, but is really a neglect of how he has commanded us to *live*? It is the difference between focusing on specific *behaviors* as opposed to a particular kind of *lifestyle*. Listen to the words of the prophet Micah.

> With what shall I come before the LORD
> and bow down before the exalted God?
> Shall I come before him with burnt offerings,
> with calves a year old?
> Will the LORD be pleased with thousands of rams,
> with ten thousand rivers of oil?
> Shall I offer my firstborn for my transgression,
> the fruit of my body for the sin of my soul?
> He has showed you, O man, what is good.
> And what does the LORD require of you?
> To act justly and to love mercy
> and to walk humbly with your God.
> —Micah 6:6–8

In this passage, specific *acts* of worship at the *personal* level (which may or may not be genuinely from the heart) take a definite back seat to a *lifestyle* at the *public* level that is committed to justice, mercy, and humility. Micah's call takes us way beyond a "me and mine" way of looking at the call of God. God requires his people to be instruments of his justice and mercy wherever he has placed them.

How you live is much more comprehensive and broader than your specific acts or roles. It is the child, the apprentice, who simply performs the duties that have been set before him. With growth and maturity comes a release into a broader world where you are expected to interact more freely with your environment. The apprentice becomes a craftsman, and the child becomes an adult. Consider the call of Christ to us all as recorded by Matthew:

> You are the light of the world. A city on a hill cannot be hidden. Neither do people light a lamp and put it under a bowl. Instead they put it on its stand, and it gives light to everyone in the house. In the same way, let your light shine before men, that they may see your good deeds and praise your Father in heaven.
>
> —Mathew 5:14–16

Jesus is saying, "You have been lit by my grace, now go let my character shine through you." How do you do this? Jesus makes it very clear: through a public life characterized by good deeds. Here again is a call to step out into this darkened world, not succumbing to thoughts of your smallness, or the magnitude of the problem, or the distance it is from your front door. It is a call to remember who you are (someone who has been lit by the transforming grace of God) and who he is (a God of awesome power and grace) and step out to look for opportunities to light what has been dark through actions of love, mercy, justice, reconciliation, peace, and compassion.

Plausible Passivity

Passivity is rarely the result of a conscious decision. You don't wake up one morning and say to yourself, "I'm going to begin to view myself as powerless. I'm going to look on God as small. So from now on, I'll just close my door and take care of me and mine." It never happens quite that way. But it does happen, all the time. Perhaps the broken-down house metaphor can help us again in illustrating the progressive stages of passivity.

One day you are walking through your living room and notice a slight crack in the wall. It is barely visible, so you think, *It's too small to worry about today*. Now, this is a perfectly plausible statement. The crack is minor and not worth re-ordering your day over. But something else also needs to be said: problems are always easiest to address when they are small. So often we make the mistake of not dealing with problems when we first notice them. After all, they crop up in the middle of the mundane moments of our lives—and we forget that those mundane moments are pretty much all we have!

You and I live in these little, mundane moments. The character of a life is not set in three or four moments of huge significance. No, the character of a life is set in 10,000 little moments, one after another. The character formed in those innumerable little moments is what positions us to respond in the big moments of life. (See the Parable of the Ten Minas, Luke 19:11–27.)

But neither the crack in your wall nor the passivity in your heart remains unchanged. So several months later your wife notices that the crack has become sizably larger. It is now very noticeable, so she asks if you would do something about it. You say, "I'll get to it when I have time." When you tell her that, you're not lying. You really do intend to fix it when you have a few free moments. The problem is that those moments never come. There is a principle here; the problems of life are not usually fixed in free and unscheduled moments. Problems generally get fixed because someone cares enough to make the time to address and solve them.

Because you haven't found that mysterious free moment in your schedule, the crack in the wall is now three inches wide at the top and runs from ceiling to floor. It has morphed from a minor to a major problem. It simply cannot be ignored any longer. At this point, however, it will take real skill to fix. So you say to yourself, *This is way too big for me to deal with.* Overwhelmed with what you're facing, you realize you're incapable of solving it.

Isn't this exactly where passivity always leads us? "Too little" and "no time" always lead to "too big."

The Call

The point of this chapter is simple but absolutely vital: you cannot think biblically and adopt a *passivity lifestyle*. To begin with, the world you live in is terribly broken (see Romans 8:18–22). Second, God's agenda is the complete renewal of everything (see Revelation 21:1–5). Third, God is sovereign and has placed you exactly where he intends for you to be (see Acts 17: 24–28). Fourth, you have been lit by God's grace and called to radiate his character in the darkness that surrounds where he has placed you (see Matthew 5:14–16, quoted previously).

The question is, will you live biblically, exercising the character and influence you have been given? Or in your passivity will you try to take yourself off the hook with self-serving rationalizations, flawed logic, and unbiblical thinking? Remember, the One who has positioned and called you is with you. To ever remind you of that fact, he has taken the name Emmanuel.

Me and Mine

Privacy fence
no sidewalks
attached garage
personal entertainment center
frenetic schedule
half acre plot
individualized
living.
Lie of autonomy
deceit of self-sufficiency
delusion of self-righteousness.
Buy your way out of
need.
Endless amusement
pushes reality out of the way.
Never known
never knowing
never stepping beyond what is
comfortable
pleasurable
enjoyable
predictable
safe.
Door closed silence,
shrunken community
of me and mine.
Thinking I can do
what I was never designed
to do,
live
all by myself.

12

Pursue Community

*I*n his hit song, "Born to Run," all Bruce Springsteen thought he needed in life was a particular girl and a fast car, a combination that must show up in a hundred other pop songs. Helen Reddy was making a political statement as well as a personal declaration of independence when she sang:

If I have to, I can do anything
I am strong
I am invincible
I am woman[1]

Down through the decades, countless songs have been built on such impassioned cries of independence, alienation, or self-reliance. Perhaps the best-known example is Frank Sinatra singing "My Way," which includes these memorable lines:

And now, the end is here
And so I face the final curtain
My friend, I'll say it clear
I'll state my case, of which I'm certain

I've lived a life that's full
I traveled each and ev'ry highway
And more, much more than this, I did it my way . . . .
For what is a man, what has he got?
If not himself, then he has naught
To say the things he truly feels and not the words of one
    who kneels
The record shows I took the blows and did it my way![2]

Of course, pop music is popular because it so powerfully captures the reigning philosophy of the culture. This desire to go it alone; the will to gut it out and make your own mark in the world; to be free, independent, and accountable to no one, runs deep in our fallen nature. It can feel really good to pretend you are completely autonomous. It can be a rich, heady experience to imagine you don't need anyone or anything else (except maybe a girl and a fast car). Indeed, this philosophy has influenced us all, even shaping the way Christians think about walking with God through this fallen world.

Look at it another way. What is the most influential, archetypal image in Western culture? Is it not the self-made man? We love the story of the guy from the wrong side of the tracks who becomes hugely successful through sheer grit and determination, and "has no one but himself to thank for it." We admire the underdog who claws his way up some impossible slope. We are fascinated by the person who emerges victorious against ridiculous odds. And no matter how much we as Christians may embrace our dependence on God, we must also admit that the way we think about our faith has been significantly shaped by the individualism of the surrounding culture.

Let's consider a couple of ways that this emphasis on individualism is playing out. In the big cities, more and more people are choosing to live alone. In the suburbs, a preference for

1. Reddy, Helen and Ray Burton. "*I Am Woman*," 1972. From the album I Am Woman (Hollywood, CA: Capital Records, 1972).

2. Anka, Paul. "My Way," 1967. First appeared on Frank Sinatra album *My Way* (Los Angeles: Reprise Records, 1969).

isolation seems to be on the rise as well. I live in downtown Philadelphia, but just outside the city, huge suburbs have been built that have no sidewalks. This is not an oversight. Community development and planning are always philosophically driven. The way we build communities reveals what is important to us. "Sidewalks? Who would use them?"

I had a friend say to me, "You know what I like about the suburbs?" Now, when you hear a question like that you just know there's something important to be learned. So I said, "No, tell me." And he said, "I love the fact that when I get in my car to go somewhere the garage door is closed behind me. I push the button to open the door, go where I need to go, come back, and I don't have to get out of the car again until the garage door is once more closed behind me."

What does my friend like about the suburbs? It goes way beyond the simple personal privacy that we all need to some degree. He loves his individualism, his solo passage through much of life, his almost perfect isolation from the very neighborhood he chose to live in! He likes the fact that he doesn't have to navigate the little "goodbye" and "hello" conversations with neighbors that are part of being in a community. He simply doesn't have to be bothered.

We all prize our right to privacy and guard our personal lives. By the time we are seven or eight years old we have learned how to put on a public persona—the version of "me" that we want people to know and love—and how to protect the details of our lives that we would rather not be publicly seen. To some degree, of course, this is healthy and normal, and helps form us as individuals. But so much of society—from popular culture, to the workings of the Internet, to the very design of our suburbs—encourages something beyond individualism. It encourages isolation and *privatism*, which one dictionary defines as "being noncommittal to or uninvolved with anything other than one's own immediate interests and lifestyle."

As I have written elsewhere, this means for many of us that we live in interwoven networks of terminally casual relationships. We live with the delusion that we know one another, but we really don't. We call our easygoing, self-protective, and often theologically platitudinous conversations "fellowship," but they seldom ever reach the threshold of true fellowship. We know cold demographic details about one another (married or single, type of job, number of kids, general location of housing, etc.), but we know little about the struggle of faith that is waged every day behind well-maintained personal boundaries.

One of the things that still shocks me in counseling, even after all these years, is how little I often know about people I have counted as true friends. I can't tell you how many times, in talking with friends who have come to me for help, that I have been hit with details of difficulty and struggle far beyond anything I would have predicted. Privatism is not just practiced by the lonely unbeliever; it is rampant in the Church as well.

Beyond "Jesus and Me"

Can any of us truly claim that our view of what it means to live as a Christian is shaped completely and exclusively by the narrative, promises, principles, and perspectives of the Word of God? No, we can't, because we are always influenced by our environment. We always drag secular culture into our faith, and this affects how we read Scripture, listen to a sermon, or evaluate the evidence of God's faithfulness. So we must always be looking for the subtle and not-so-subtle ways that cultural assumptions have twisted how we think about and live out our faith.

We must face up to the fact that we have been influenced by the individualism and privatism of our culture, and that this influence can take a great many forms. Tim has harbored doubts about the love of God for years, but no one knows.

Sarah's three children under age five drive her to the edge of insanity, but no one is aware. Bill has said things to his teenager he would never want anyone else to hear about, and probably no one will. Anita's world is increasingly full of fear and dread, but nobody has a clue. Frank and Bonnie had another violent argument yesterday, but no one will find out. Jared once again visited shameful Internet sites last night, but not even his wife knows of his struggle. Jenny's decades-old bitterness toward her mom and dad has shaped every relationship in her life, but no one is even aware there's a problem. John's private world is one of consumption and debt, but his secret is well hidden. After her boyfriend walked away, Kimmy quit reading her Bible and praying, but she hasn't told anybody. Peter's Christianity has become a system of impossible-to-keep, guilt-producing rules, but he is afraid to admit it out loud.

Under the influence of Western culture, Christianity tends to take on a uniquely individualistic cast, a "Jesus and me" kind of faith. We talk much about a "personal relationship with Jesus." And it is certainly true that we are brought, by God's grace, into personal communion with Christ. But Christianity is equally a faith that is meant to be anchored in community.

Listen to the covenant promise made to Abram:

"I will make you into a great nation
  and I will bless you;
I will make your name great,
  and you will be a blessing.
I will bless those who bless you,
  and whoever curses you I will curse;
and all peoples on earth
  will be blessed through you."
—Genesis 12:2–3

This wasn't just some private pact between Abram and God. No, God was calling Abram to be part of *a people*. God's purpose in working through Abram's life was corporate. He was raising up *a people* upon whom he would place his name and to whom he would show his grace. What we need to see is that *a people* is not just a collection of individuals. Individuals collect at a gate to catch a plane on Tuesday. But it is *a people* who gather to worship God on Sunday.

God's call to a people has its roots in Genesis 2, where we see that God has designed human beings to live in community, first with him and then with one another. When we read in Genesis 2:18, "It is not good for man to be alone," these words are not the lonely cry of Adam, but spoken by God as an expression of his creative design. From the outset, God designed men and women to be social beings. We only fulfill this particular intent of our Designer when we live in worshipful community with God and interdependent community with other human beings. If community was vital in the perfect world before sin bent and twisted us and our surroundings, how much more vital is it now that we live in this broken-down house!

Reflect with me on this summary of God's redemptive purpose in Jesus Christ, "who gave himself for us to redeem us from all wickedness and to purify for himself *a people* that are his very own, eager to do what is good" (Titus 2:14, emphasis mine). Paul doesn't speak about the work of Christ in the individualistic way we often do. He recognizes that, although God is calling individuals to himself, he is gathering them together in order to form a "people for his own possession." The "Jesus and me" religion of modern Christianity is not the Christianity of the Bible. We have privatized and individualized a faith that is distinctly and inextricably rooted both in vertical community (between God and his people) and in horizontal community (among groups of Christians).

Remembering Is a Community Project

In Chapter 3 we examined the importance of living out of a biblical sense of identity, the two central components of that identity being that I am a *sinner*, and at the same time, a *child of grace*. Only when I hold these identities in their proper balance and tension can I ever be and do what God has designed and called me to be and do. Yet it is so easy either to emphasize one identity to the neglect of the other, or live as if I have forgotten them both. Because it's true that these identities really are an accurate picture of who I am in God, holding onto them is one of my most important spiritual battles. This is where biblical community comes in.

In this fallen world, where falsehood wars against truth and reality battles with delusion, it is hard to remember who I am. When I look into the perfect mirror of the Word of God I see myself accurately and am confronted with my true identity: sinner, yet child of grace. But there are other, less reliable, mirrors I look into as well.

Sometimes I see myself in the carnival mirror of culture and its twisted image of what a successful human being looks like. Sometimes I see myself in the distorted mirror of my own self-righteousness, portraying me as more godly and mature than I actually am. Sometimes I see myself in the crazy funhouse mirror, which is the overly positive appraisal of well-intentioned friends. Sometimes I see myself in the cracked mirror of daily home life, where what God emphasizes as important is not always practiced. Each of these mirrors offers a representation of me, but with crucial and unbiblical distortions that can drive me to make unbiblical, sinful, harmful decisions.

So, with the tendency to identity distortion within and the danger of it without, I need help remembering who I really am. If I receive that help, I can live with a more cogent awareness of sin and grace, with radically different results than if I seek to live this inherently communitarian life on my own.

I will only know myself accurately when I know myself in biblical community. My walk with God really is a community project.

The Call to Biblical Community

Many passages in the New Testament call us to practice biblical community, but I want to look at two that are particularly powerful. The first is Hebrews 3:12–13. "See to it, brothers, that none of you has a sinful, unbelieving heart that turns away from the living God. But encourage one another daily, as long as it is called Today, so that none of you may be hardened by sin's deceitfulness." I have commented extensively on this passage in other books, so I won't do so here. Rather, I want to focus on the struggle and the solution we find embedded in the passage.

The *struggle* is revealed in our need for daily mutual encouragement, without which we can become hardened and turn away from God. As long as I am a sinner living in this fallen world, it will be impossible to see myself with anything approaching perfect accuracy. In fact, left to myself, I will only tend to become more and more deceived. It is time that we gave up the delusion that we have anything like the accurate perspective on ourselves that we think we do. It is time we humbly admit that our view of ourselves is blurred by the distorted lens of our own sin and the assortment of faulty mirrors we encounter daily in the culture. Sure, as you mature in your faith you will gradually come to see yourself more accurately, but as long as sin still lives in your heart there will be significant distortions in your self-perspective.

But this passage also holds out the *solution* to our struggle. It is a solution both humbling and frightening: I must come to admit that I desperately need the very people I can work so hard to hide from. The powerful truth found in this passage is that personal spiritual insight—an accurate knowledge of self—can *only* come when I am actively engaged in community.

You can't get it any other way! It's true that this insight cannot be achieved without the ministry of the Holy Spirit in your heart, but this Spirit upon whom you and I depend happens to be telling us in this passage that he uses instruments: one another. My tendency to personal blindness is so deep and pervasive that I need the intervention of other Christians who know me. What's more, I need them "as long as it is called Today"—in other words, every day! In protecting myself from other people, I only keep myself from knowing me. I keep myself from seeing myself with the accuracy that produces a God-honoring life in the middle of a terribly broken world.

The second passage is equally powerful. It is also from the book of Hebrews:

> Therefore, brothers, since we have confidence to enter the Most Holy Place by the blood of Jesus, by a new and living way opened for us through the curtain, that is, his body, and since we have a great priest over the house of God, let us draw near to God with a sincere heart in full assurance of faith, having our hearts sprinkled to cleanse us from a guilty conscience and having our bodies washed with pure water. Let us hold unswervingly to the hope we profess, for he who promised is faithful.
>
> And let us consider how we may spur one another on toward love and good deeds. Let us not give up meeting together, as some are in the habit of doing, but let us encourage one another—and all the more as you see the Day approaching.
>
> If we deliberately keep on sinning after we have received the knowledge of the truth, no sacrifice for sins is left, but only a fearful expectation of judgment and of raging fire that will consume the enemies of God. Anyone who rejected the law of Moses died without mercy on the testimony of two or three witnesses. How much more severely do you think a man deserves to be punished who has trampled the Son of God under foot, who has treated as an unholy thing the blood of the covenant that sanctified him, and who has insulted the Spirit of grace? For we know him who said, "It is mine to avenge; I will repay,"

and again, "The Lord will judge his people." It is a dreadful
thing to fall into the hands of the living God.
                    —Hebrews 10:19–31(passage divisions mine)

The flow of this passage is a bit curious until you focus in
on what it is saying. It falls into three distinct parts. Verses
19–23 contain one of the New Testament's clearest calls to live
with the courage and confidence that can only come when you
acknowledge your identity as a *child of grace*. This section talks
of drawing near to God in "full assurance of faith." It calls
us to "hold unswervingly to the hope we profess," being sure
that "he who promised is faithful." It is a call to live where
the rubber meets the road in your daily life—as if you really
do believe that you have been given, by God's grace, a whole
new identity, and with it a bright new potential.

Let's skip ahead to the third section of the passage, verses
26–31. These verses involve my identity as a *sinner*, and contain one of the Bible's strongest calls to be serious about sin.
Phrases about trampling the Son of God under foot, insulting
the Spirit of grace, and falling dreadfully into the hands of
the living God alert me to how seriously I should view the sin
that lives within me and is so easy to give way to. It's true:
every time you and I minimize, justify, rationalize, or explain
away our sin, we insult the Spirit of grace. This is the same
Holy Spirit who controlled the course of history so that at
the right time the Son of God would come to suffer and die.
Why? To deliver us from the sin that we can suggest is really
not all that important!

Now, back to the middle section of this powerful passage.
Between part one, an encouragement to grasp boldly the
resources available to me as a *child of grace*, and part three,
a call to live in humble recognition of myself as a *sinner*,
appear two little verses. At first glance they don't seem to fit
the context. What are these two verses about community doing
in the middle of this discussion on identity? The word "us" is
certainly peppered through this whole passage, but why this

mention of the obviously collective, interdependent "us" in a passage that seems to be about "us" as simply a number of individuals? What is the church-as-a-unity doing in here, when otherwise this section seems basically to be about the identity of me, the reader?

Go back and read again verses 19–23, and then verses 24–25, and notice what happens. As we get to verses 24–25 we stop looking straight ahead, as if we are marching to a glorious destination in God all by ourselves. Instead, we turn our heads to the right and to the left, and we realize there are brothers and sisters with whom we are marching and upon whom we are desperately dependent. That reality and the message of these two verses couldn't be more important to those of us who have been chosen by God to live as Christians in this broken-down house.

The point of that middle section is clear. There is only one way you and I will ever hold onto the two identities—*child of grace*, yet *sinner*—that propel a godly life in this fallen and idolatrous world. It can only happen when we are living in functional, biblical community with people who will again and again remind us of who we are. I need people in my life who will lovingly hold the mirror of the Word of God in front of me so that I can see how deep my struggle with sin still is. I need people who will confront my timidity and avoidance with the comforting, encouraging, emboldening realities of faith: I am a child of the amazing grace of Emmanuel, God ever with me. I was not wired to walk this walk of faith by myself. I was not created and then recreated to live on my own. I must admit to my constant tendency to minimize both the grace I have been given and the sin that is the reason I need it so. I must face the fact that many times I simply forget who I am.

The central lesson of this passage is that we need one another daily in order to avoid identity amnesia. Yet we have essentially reduced the passage to a single command: "Make sure you go to church on Sunday." Faithful church attendance is certainly part of this passage, but it is also a call to much, much more. It is a call to community that is *intentionally intrusive*, *Christ-centered*, *grace-driven*, and *redemptive*. Let me take apart this phrase for you.

Intentionally intrusive means I have invited fellow Christians to intrude into the private spaces of my life in order to help me see myself with biblical accuracy. This does not mean I gush out my sin to everyone who comes my way. That wouldn't be helpful to anyone. But I must be in some kind of web of godly, intentional relationships that can produce the personal insight I so desperately need.

Christ-centered means that the hope and goal of these relationships is Christ. We do not build these relationships for self-centered purposes. Personal happiness and fulfillment are byproducts of a healthy Christian life, but they cannot be the focus. We pursue such relationships because we know how much we need Christ and we know that what we offer one another is not just *our love*, but *his grace*.

Grace-driven means we do not try to function as private detectives or self-appointed prosecutors. The purpose of the relationship is not to *catch* the other person doing wrong, but to motivate and encourage him or her to do what is right. We minister to one another knowing that while the law is able to reveal sin, only grace can deliver us from it!

Redemptive relationships means we recognize that change is a process, not a quick leap to sinless perfection. We *have been* redeemed, we *are being* redeemed, and we *will be* redeemed. We love God and one another enough to want to be part of the good that God is doing in that person's life right here, right now, even though sin still remains, and sometimes quite obviously. We reject the selfish "I love you and have a wonderful plan for your life" agenda that causes us to turn fellow Christians into personal projects. Instead, we have taken up God's agenda of radical personal change for ourselves, change so fundamental that it causes rebels like you and me to become "partakers of [his] divine nature" (2 Peter 1:4, ESV).

No More Hiding

Let me suggest you take a moment right now and be perfectly honest with yourself as you answer this question:

Are you still hiding?

Don't let yourself weasel out of it by rationalizing that no one is ever perfectly, completely transparent. That wasn't the question. With the help of your conscience, you probably know exactly what I mean. Are there fellow Christians in your life who you are confident, and rightly so, that they are aware of the major areas of spiritual difficulty and temptation in your life, and you are willing to discuss these areas with them in ways that are open and helpful? After more than two decades in ministry, I have to say with sadness that unless you are part of a very small minority among Christians in this culture, your honest answer is probably no.

Could the fact that you are still hiding explain why there are struggles you can't seem to get consistently under control? Are you still holding onto the belief that you really do know yourself better than anyone else? Are you still imagining that you are wiser, more sanctified, and spiritually stronger than you actually are?

It is time to face the fact that your walk with God is a community project. It is time to come out of hiding. The Christians around you struggle just like you, and the God who is your hope is not surprised by your struggle or theirs. He knows every challenge and temptation of your heart. That's why he sent his Son to live, die, and rise again.

Step out of where you are hiding and into the kind of community that Scripture clearly says you need. Where will you find that intentionally intrusive, Christ-centered, grace-driven, redemptive community?

You're not designed to live without it. Life in this broken-down house really is a community project.

You Are Not Like Me

I am good at it,
a skill
I don't think I ever
had to learn.
It resides in my
heart.
It is an anti-social
instinct,
but it shapes my
relationships.
I am able to look at
people
and not see
people.
My craving
heart
reduces them to
vehicles that deliver or
obstacles in the way
of what I want.
My only
hope
for me is that
You are not like me.
You are
Love
and You are
delivering
me from me.

13

Determine to Love

Honestly, I cannot recall a single day where I have not encountered evidence of the Fall. And if I could fast-forward through a video recording of my life, I doubt I would even find an hour without such evidence. In countless ways, you and I are continually confronted with the brokenness surrounding us and within us. It has been this way through all of human history. It is the reason that people everywhere have always agreed, "life is hard."

Perhaps it's the pain that greets you as you get out of bed. Maybe it's the reality that you are facing another holiday without that loved one who always made the season so special. Perhaps it's the latest natural disaster that has devastated entire communities and swallowed up lives. It may be the hurtful thing a good friend said to you yesterday evening. Or maybe you're just tired of hearing about wars, disease, political corruption, urban violence, racism, Internet pornography, and a seemingly endless catalog of ills that daily alert you to the fact that you really do live in a groaning and broken-down house.

But there is another truth at work here as well, something else that you must face up to: it is not an accident that you are right here, right now. God has chosen and arranged for you to live precisely where and when you are living. It can be hard to grasp, but the God who is the ultimate source of wisdom, power, and love has exercised all three of these limitless attributes to place you where you are today. In Acts 17 Paul says of God that "he himself gives all men life and breath and everything else . . . and he determined the times set for them and the exact places where they should live" (vv. 25–26). God chose for me to be alive in this period of history. He alone determines the day of my death. And he decided exactly where I would live!

This means God has a reason and a purpose for me, here and now, in this broken-down house of a world. His wisdom and intentionality are at work in my life and in yours. Yet I think this is the point where we often lose our way: the harsh realities of the fallen world can tempt us to question God's wisdom, or love, or power, or all three.

The hardships we face often don't make sense to us. We find ourselves swept up in something far bigger than we are—a global economic crisis, for example—and it can seem like a vast system of unrelated, impersonal forces is actually affecting the world in a random way, instead of a loving and omnipotent God ruling the world in a purposeful way. The collection of large and small difficulties that make up so much of our lives can seem like pointless obstacles blocking our access to the good life God has promised us.

It is admittedly difficult to greet hardships as a testimony to God's wisdom, power, and love, but that is exactly what they are. The only reason we find it hard is because the "good" we seek and hope for is different from the good that God is accomplishing through the difficulties that come our way.

Often when we look back on a "good" week, we think it was good because it was comfortable, predictable, pleasurable, controllable, successful, etc. Our evaluation of the week is shaped by our wants, feelings, and estimation of our needs. But there is another "good" that God is working on. He is using this period of time to continue the work of radical rescue and restoration that he has begun in us.

There is yet more work God desires to do in our lives before we go to spend eternity with him. God does not settle for "good enough." He loves us too much to sit back idly while we struggle with personal weakness, failure, and sin. He is not satisfied to leave us at the level of immaturity and foolishness we find ourselves in today. He has a character goal for you to attain in this life, and by his unrelenting grace and mercy you are going to get there. He is God. We are made in his likeness. His ultimate goal for us in this life is that we be further conformed to his image. So he will not stop doing good to us—good in the most important sense of the term, however painful it may be at times—for as long as we are on this earth.

A Time of Preparation

What does this mean for the here and now? It means this is not a time of slogging through hardships day after day, just hoping they will end soon. Yes, we wait for the day when our hardships will be over. Waiting and hoping are biblical and legitimate. But the issue for now is not the future. The issue for now is *now*. The question is not, "When will we get what we are waiting for?" but "What we will *become* as we wait?" Passages like Romans 5 and 8, James 1, and 1 Peter 1 remind us that God is not just working on bringing things to a final end. He is working *on us*! The agenda during this moment is not *destination*, but *preparation*; not "How can I get the good stuff ASAP?" but "How is God working to change me *now* in anticipation of *then*?"

Preparation is hard. Any athlete will tell you that competing is more fun than training. Yet all successful athletes put themselves through self-imposed torture because they recognize the vital importance of preparation. The hours in the gym, the early morning runs, the repetitive drills, the careful diet, the costly expenditures of time and money, the sacrifice of other pleasures, the mental discipline, and the willing submission to the wisdom and authority of coaches are simply some of the rigors of careful preparation.

My son, Darnay, has a friend who played college football. We have known him since he was a small boy. I remember his puny little-boy body when he was in Pee Wee Football. Then we watched as he and his family got serious about his football. There were many times when Darnay wanted to do something with his friend, but he was in the gym lifting weights, or out running. We watched as he became more and more successful, even receiving a college scholarship. But what I remember most is how he changed physically. Over time, the weightlifting and exercise he did literally remolded his body. No longer was he the skinny kid I had once known. With lots of muscle mass and minimal body fat, he barely resembled that boy who had grown up around us. Not only was his body larger and stronger, he was faster and more limber, far more versatile and agile than ever before. His body, mind, and reflexes had honed themselves into a single, formidable tool. He had become what he needed to be so that he might enjoy success in the sport he had chosen.

This a lot like what God is doing in you through the hardships you encounter. There is a point to the daily drills and the grueling exercises you face. They are not random or pointless bouts of pain, temptation, and challenge. God is training and changing you in mind, body, and spirit. He is building you up from frailty, immaturity, and weakness, and making you capable in areas where before you could only dream of success. Where your spirit tends to be slow, selfish, and lethargic, he is developing in you new reflexes and habit patterns of love and service to others. He is building onto you the muscle-mass of godliness to increase your spiritual strength and stamina. His intention is to rebuild you so fundamentally that you no longer resemble the person you once were. And he wants to teach you how to use this new set of abilities for the thing to which he has called you—service in his kingdom of glory and grace.

So What's Love Got to Do with It?

Perhaps you're reading along and you're thinking, "But, Paul, I thought this was a chapter on love and all you're talking about is the hardship of being chosen by God to live and mature in this broken-down house. I'm lost." Well, here's the connection. It has to do with the fact that the basic condition of hardship that you face in life—the pain and difficulty and challenge and uncertainty—is also faced in various ways by everyone else on the planet.

So let me say it again: life in this fallen world is hard. Preparation is hard. Change is hard. It is very easy to get discouraged. It is very easy to feel overwhelmed. It is very easy to remain or revert to being self-focused and self-absorbed. It is very easy to feel alone. It is very easy to think that no one understands what you are going through. It is very easy to think that God must have gotten a wrong address; that this trial couldn't have been intended for your doorstep. It is very easy to give in to wondering if following God is worth it. It is very easy to look over the fence and yield to debilitating envy. It is very easy to begin to let go of good and godly habits. It is very easy to try to numb or distract yourself by whatever temporary pleasure is within reach. It is very easy to try to convince yourself that you are godlier than you are and therefore less in need of change than you actually are. It is very easy to hit those moments when you lose your way and just want to give up. Life in the fallen world is hard.

That is why God, in his love, has designed for us not to be left in this broken-down house alone, but to live here with others in a community of love. When I read 1 Peter 1, I am always struck by how God has placed a call to love at the end of a discussion of hardship. As Peter summarizes what God is doing in the here and now he uses three words, "suffer, grief, and trial." None of us want these things in our lives! But Peter reminds us that they have come our way as tools of refinement in the hands of a loving Redeemer, intent on completing in us what he has begun. Then Peter begins to lay out how to live productively in the middle of the hardships of the here and now.

Listen to his final directive, "Now that you have purified yourselves by obeying the truth so that you have sincere love for your brothers, love one another deeply, from the heart" (1 Peter 1: 22). Peter is saying something very powerful here. He is saying that God hasn't simply called us to endure the refining fires of sanctification. He has ordained us to incarnate his love through the community of love he has placed around us. This community of love is meant not only to give us hope and strength, but to encourage us with a reminder that the One who is testing and training us is with us and loves us.

This community of love is meant to comfort the person who is discouraged, to strengthen the person who is weak, to give hope to the person who has none, to be present with the person who is alone, to guide the person who has lost his way, to give wisdom to the person lost in foolishness, to warn the person who is beginning to wander, to correct the person turning the wrong way, to give eyes to the person who is blind to God's presence, and to be a physical representation of God's presence and love.

So, as you are living in the broken-down house, what does God call you to do? There is one sure and reliable answer to the question: he calls you to be an instrument of his love.

There is no lack in your life for opportunities to love. That teenager who is growingly attracted to the world needs God's love. That single person who is facing the death of personal dreams needs God's love. That immigrant brother or sister who feels so out of place and so misunderstood needs God's love. That mom who is simply overwhelmed with her parenting responsibilities needs God's love. That man who is tempted to walk out of his troubled marriage needs God's love. That little boy who lost his father to divorce needs God's love. That woman who is living through the ravages of cancer needs God's love. That couple facing debts they don't seem able to pay needs God's love. The woman who now faces life without the man who has been her companion for decades needs God's love. That pastor carrying a heavy weight of spiritual responsibility needs God's love. That university student facing the spiritual warfare of college needs God's love.

We could multiply example after example. There is no location, situation, or relationship this side of heaven where this love is not needed. This love is not about liking people. It is not about romantic affection. It is something more than cultural niceness. It is deeper than being respectful or mannerly. This love finds its motivation, hope, and direction at the cross of Jesus Christ.

The Shape of Love

What is the nature and shape of the love to which each of us has been called? Hear the words of 1 John 4:9–11.

> This is how God showed his love among us: He sent his one and only Son into the world that we might live through him. This is love; not that we loved God, but that he loved us and sent his Son as an atoning sacrifice for our sins. Dear friends, since God so loved us, we ought to love one another.

169

What is our motivation to love others? We love others because we have been so magnificently loved. Jesus said, when the woman washed his feet with expensive perfume and dried them with her hair, "The one who is forgiven much, loves much." We live with a deep sense of privilege that, quite apart from anything we could earn, deserve, or achieve, our lives have been transformed by the love of God. He has every reason to turn his back on us. He has every reason to turn his anger against us. He has every reason to judge us unworthy, but he does not. He first turns to us so that we would then turn to him. So, being filled with the awe of this love, we are excited about sharing this love with others. And we really do believe that this love is the most powerful force for change in the universe.

What is the hope of this love? We don't feel burdened by this call to love, because we know that the God, who is love, is transforming us by his love, so that we will increasingly be people who love. Here is the biblical model: *God's love rescues us from self-love so that we will be able to love others.* Let me unpack this for you.

God knows that, because we are sinners, our first inclination is not to love others, but to love ourselves. Sin turns us in on ourselves. Sin causes us to be selfish, self-absorbed, and self-focused. Sin causes us to be obsessed with what we want, what we feel, and what we think we need. Sin causes us to want to exist at the center of our own universe, having our feelings addressed, our wants satisfied, and our needs met. Sin makes us demanding and expectant, rather than serving and giving. So God has to rescue us from us. He has to free us from our bondage to ourselves so that we can live for him and for others. And as he does this, God is not taking our humanity from us. He is giving it back to us. You see, we were designed to love him and to love others. In progressively freeing us from sin, he is increasingly enabling us to live as we were created to live. And this is itself the happiest and most satisfying way to live.

God has arranged all this so that we need not be overwhelmed or weighed down with the call to love, for the God who *is* love now lives inside of us empowering us to love others as he has loved us. But there is more.

We don't have to wonder what in the world this love is meant to look like. We don't have to fear that we won't know how to function as his tools of love. Why? Because there is a moment in history that is the final definition of the love to which God has called us. That moment is the cross of Jesus Christ. We have been called to *cruciform* love. What does this mean? This means that the love we give to others must shape itself, mold itself, to resemble in some essential way what took place at the cross of the Lord Jesus Christ. Hear these words again, "since God so loved us, we ought also to love one another."

What does this cross-shaped love look like in the hallways, subways, boardrooms, living rooms, and sidewalks of everyday life? It looks like what Jesus did for us. Here is what this love is. Here is how it functions. It is *willing self-sacrifice for the redemptive good of another.*

It is *willing.* No one took Jesus' life from him; he laid it down himself as an act of his own will. God calls us to be willing and ready to function as instruments of his love.

It requires *sacrifice.* For Jesus, this meant his death. It is not likely to mean death for you or me, although it might. What is important to recognize, however, is the element of costliness. Love is costly. There is no such thing as true, active love that does not require sacrifice. God calls us to be willing to lay down our lives; to be willing to sacrifice time, energy, money, reputation, possessions—whatever may be necessary as we seek to love others as we have been loved.

And we do all of this for the *redemptive good* of others. Jesus died so that salvation would be accomplished and transforming grace would be available. The cross guarantees that someday all of God's children will be finally free of every last microbe of sin in every last cell of their hearts. So we look for opportunities to be part of what God is doing in the lives of others and we will not stop looking until all of God's work is completed in all of his children.

This call to love is second only to our call to worship God above anything else. And if this has been God's will from the beginning, before the Fall, how much more is it needed as we live under the burdens of life in a broken world!

Cruciform Love in the Here and Now

Let me suggest in very functional, practical terms what it means to be committed to being an instrument of cross-shaped love:

It means not keeping yourself so busy with you and yours that you have no practical time to love others.

It means being committed to knowing people, because you can minister only in very limited ways to those whom you do not know.

It means being willing to have your life complicated by the needs and struggles of others.

It means being willing to share your physical resources with others.

It means being willing to live with an open home.

It means being perseverant and patient even when the love you give is not returned.

It means actively looking for places where you can function as one of God's tools of love.

It means resisting the temptation to be judgmental, self-righteous, and critical.

It means overlooking minor offenses and fighting the temptation to become bitter or cynical.

It means making life decisions out of a recognition of this inescapable call to love.

It means being lovingly and humbly honest in moments of misunderstanding; more committed to reconciliation than to being right.

It means admitting that you are still learning to love as you have been loved.

It means being willing to own up to your sin and admit your faults.

It means not judging the success of your life by the size of your house or bank account, or by the quality of your car, but by the quality of your love for God and others.

It means regularly examining the motivations, desires, and thoughts of your heart in the mirror of God's Word.

It means moving beyond simply surrounding yourself with people whom you find comfortable and likeable.

It means being a student of God's Word, a joyful participant in the means of grace, and a committed participant in the fellowship of the body of Christ, so that the love you offer others may be increasingly pure and mature.

It means being willing to be misunderstood, mistreated, and misrepresented for the sake of incarnating Christ's love.

It means overcoming evil with good.

It means not letting race, social class, gender, age, or ethnicity get in the way of a biblical call to Christlike love.

It means being willing to have your schedule and plans interrupted or altered.

It means being willing to grant and seek forgiveness.

It means paying attention to the physical, emotional, and spiritual needs of the people God puts in your path, and looking for ways to help them bear these burdens.

It means believing that God will not call you to a task without giving you what you need to accomplish it.

It means being willing to get up earlier and stay up later.

It means learning the details about someone's struggle so that you can love wisely, while at the same time guarding the reputation of the person you are loving.

It means weeping with the one who weeps and rejoicing with the one who rejoices.

It means being willing to endure tense and uncomfortable situations lovingly.

It means not allowing yourself plausible excuses that seemingly free you from love's call.

It means making a commitment to being a faithful friend.

It means being willing to take on big things, even as you humbly admit your limits.

It means keeping your promises and being faithful to your word.

It means being open to correction, loving criticism, and godly rebuke.

It means believing in the body of Christ and recognizing that you are but one of the tools in God's big toolbox of redemption.

It means being open to counsel and receptive to advice.

It means being willing to go to bed tired and to awake to another day of calling.

It means hiding God's Word in your heart and keeping his Kingdom always before your eyes.

It means refusing to become anyone's substitute messiah, but instead to point people to the presence and grace of Jesus.

It really does mean looking out not only for your own interests, but also for the interests of others.

It means building relationships, not just for the purpose of being relationally comfortable, but so that those relationships would be a workroom for redemption.

It means loving people in such a way that they never feel like they are in debt to you.

It means remembering that you are more like than unlike the people you are called to love.

It means understanding that the call to love is a call to both word and deed.

It means daily remembering Jesus, being in awe of the gift of his love, and living thankfully.

Someone near you right now has lost his way. Someone near you is feeling alone. Someone near you is overwhelmed. Someone near you is being tempted to step off God's pathway.

Someone near you is doubting God's presence and love. The God who is love now lives inside of you, enabling you to love as you have been loved. He has chosen you to be one of his ambassadors, incarnating his love in the lives of those he has placed you near. Open your eyes and your heart and offer to others what you have been given. There is no better way to live in this fallen world.

Celebration

It will be
the most exuberant
celebration ever.
It will never grow
boring.
It will always be
fresh
It will consume us all.
We will want to do
nothing else.
The celebration will go
on and on,
with songs that will never grow
old.
We will be so amazed
that we have been invited into
the choir.
And our amazement will never
abate.
This celebration that will never
end
is the celebration of
grace.
If you listen carefully
You will hear
the songs have already
begun.

14

Celebrate Grace

*I*t should be the thing that greets your mind and fills your heart as you wake each morning. It should be your final thought as you settle in for a night of sleep. It should define how you face your day, and it should shape your self-reflections. It should be the thing that directs how you respond to others. It should be at the forefront of your thoughts in times of trouble or disappointment. It should alter how you think about finances, possessions, decisions, relationships, and everything else. It should be a central theme of your existence. It is so huge, so gorgeous, and so glorious that once it gets hold of you, you will never be the same again.

You don't need to be an expert at riddles for this one. I am talking about *grace*.

If you are God's child, grace is the stunning core reality of your existence. It is the most amazing thing that has ever happened to you, or ever will. It has changed everything you have, do, and are. It has redefined your past, refocused your present, and reshaped your future. It is the thing that you have needed since your first breath. It is an absolutely essential ingredient of productive living on this side of eternity. It is what you and I will focus on and celebrate for the rest of eternity. And it is vital that in preparation for eternity we start our celebration now.

Playing with the Box

Luella and I gave birth to a son who didn't understand what to do with gifts. We would shop for what we thought was just the right gift for him. Then on Christmas, or his birthday, we would watch as he gleefully tore open the wrapping. But not long afterward we would find him playing with the box, his carefully chosen gift lying neglected on the floor! This went on for years, and eventually became quite frustrating.

One Christmas, Luella and I decided to find our son a gift he simply could not resist. After extensive shopping, we found it. Both of us realized at the same moment that this was the perfect choice. We were certain that this was a gift he would actually play with.

Christmas morning arrived, and we were all sitting around the tree opening our gifts. I'm sure Luella and I were gripped by more anticipation than our son was. We couldn't wait for the moment when he opened that particular gift, couldn't wait to see the look on his face. We just knew that this gift would truly capture his attention. Finally the gift was in front of him, and his little hands instantly shredded the wrapping. He saw the box, opened the box, removed the toy, and actually began playing with it! With the toy! I was filled with a warm feeling of parental accomplishment.

I went into the kitchen to get something to drink. When I returned to the living room a few minutes later, the toy was there on the floor, and our son was sitting in the box! I couldn't believe it! We had given him the best toy ever and he was still quite content to play with the box.

Why am I telling you this cute family story? Because I'm convinced that many Christians are a lot like my son. You and I have been given the best gift that could ever be given.

However closely you study it, from whatever perspective you choose to examine it, it is astonishing and gorgeous and awesome in the true sense of the word. No other gift could possibly be more significant or life-changing. As an act of sheer, breathtaking, over-the-top generosity and kindness, no other gift comes close.

The gift of grace is the single most important thing every human being needs. And we all need it equally; no one needs it more, and no one needs it less. Without this gift you will never be what you were designed to be, or do what you were created to do. It is a gift you could never earn, achieve, or deserve. It has the power to completely transform you and everything you desire, choose, think, say, and do. It is the gift of gifts. It is the gift of the grace of the Lord Jesus Christ. But I am deeply persuaded that many Christians, having been given this awesome gift, are content to play with the box.

We are content with episodic Christianity, a faith that lives most vibrantly on Sunday morning. We are content with stepping out of our busy schedules for occasional participation in ministry. We are content with a little bit of casual fellowship (which, being casual, usually is not fellowship at all). We are content with putting a little bit of money in the offering plate. We may support and encourage the ministry of others, but if someone were to watch a video of our lives they would quickly conclude we are driven by hopes, dreams, and values that have little or nothing to do with God's purposes. Sadly, having been given the most wonderful and transformative gift that could ever be, I think there are many Christians who are quite content to play with the box.

Now, there is a principle underneath this reality. *The things that you say to you about you will determine how you hold onto God's gift of grace.* A life-shaping celebration of God's grace is only ever born out of one thing: a deep sense of profound personal need. Do you remember the Pharisee in Christ's story as he prayed in the temple? (Luke 18:9–14). Do you remember his prayer? "God, I thank you that I am not like other men—robbers, evildoers, adulterers—or even like this tax collector. I fast twice a week, and I give a tenth of what I get." As I mentioned earlier, this man was essentially saying, "God, I don't need you because, frankly, I am okay." Do you see that what this man said *to* himself *about* himself removed from him any sense that he actually needed the God to whom he was praying? Listen to Luke's set-up of this brief parable. "To some who were *confident of their own righteousness* and looked down on everybody else, Jesus told this parable" (emphasis mine). Self-righteousness never promotes a daily pursuit and celebration of grace.

The only reason we can be content playing with the box is that we have convinced ourselves we are okay in ourselves, that we are self-sufficient, that where we are in God right now is good enough. Sure, in some abstract way we believe that sin still resides within us, but as we look around we can identify lots of people spiritually worse off than us. You see, in many of us a process takes hold that is terribly debilitating spiritually. It goes like this: the longer we walk with the Lord, and the longer we participate in some way in the life and ministry of the church, the more self-assured we can become. We begin to lose our sense of need. We begin to think of ourselves as one of the good guys. Like the Pharisee, we begin to look down on others, who we see as the "real sinners." We begin to think we have actually arrived. No longer do we come to worship God with a heartfelt sense of need and anticipation. No longer do we hunger for the sustenance and rescue that the Word of God can give us. No longer do we feel the need for the regular fellowship of the body of Christ, which is meant to remind us of our ongoing struggle and the new identity we have been given in Christ. No longer do we seek out every opportunity to share this extraordinary gift with someone who has either forgotten it or not yet received it.

Having convinced ourselves that we are righteous in ourselves, we are content to play with the box. We're not holding onto God's gift of grace with both hands, refusing to let go until it has done everything it was given to do in us and through us. We're not refusing to let go until every microbe of sin had been completely eradicated from every cell of our hearts. We're not holding on until every thought, every desire, every motive, every choice, every word, and every action of our lives is completely in line with God's plan and purpose. We're not holding on until his Word really is hidden in our hearts and transforming the way we think and live. We're not holding on until it can be finally said of us, echoing 1 Peter 1:16, "They are holy as God is holy."

We have lost our sense of need, and in losing our sense of need, we have lost our sense of urgency, and in losing our sense of urgency, we have lost our zeal. When this happens, our living is no longer shaped by a celebration of the awesome gift of grace that we have been given. No, grace gets reduced to an aspect of an aspect of our lives. Our Christianity gets assigned to the religious dimension of our lives, and when this happens our lives begin to be shaped by a different sense of need, and along with it a different set of hopes, dreams, and values.

What's Your Dream?

What you dream for, what you hope for, what you work for, what you make strategic life decisions to pursue, and what you celebrate when received will all be determined by what you tell yourself you need the most. I am shocked as I hear Christians throw around the word "need," shocked at how little of our conversation has anything whatsoever to do with our profound need of grace. It's amazing that the one thing we need the most doesn't even make the list of things we say we need! We are convinced we need a spouse, a better job, a nicer home, more friends, a better church, better health, a new couch, and on and on. None of these things are wrong to desire, but if need means "essential to life," then these are not needs.

You would think that at the top of everyone's needs list would be those things that really are essential for life. None of the things I just listed, and frankly very few of our material "needs," are actually essential for life. But grace is. Grace is absolutely essential for every moment of our lives. It is essential in the small and unnoticed things like your next breath and your next heartbeat, and it is essential for the great long-term goals and plans of your life that God established before the foundation of the world.

But what do we do? We tend to take that long list of needs—for ultimately we all are desperately needy creatures, whether we realize it or not—and when it comes to those items that are truly essential, because God is so kind and has established such a stable and wonderful existence for us, many of these essential needs we just take for granted. We don't talk about our need for water because we trust it's going to be there. We don't talk about our need for gravity because we trust it's going to be there. Most of us reading this book don't talk about our need for a society free of anarchy, because we trust in there being a fairly stable social order. So those things may be some of the most essential items on our needs list, but because we take them for granted we just cross them off, and end up skipping well down the list before we come to something we *don't already have*: a nicer couch, a better body-fat ratio, or a car that runs a little better than the one we currently drive. So those are the things we talk about. And at the very *top* of that list of essential things we have taken for granted, above all the other essential things we've crossed out because they are already reliable, we have also crossed out item number one: the grace of God. After all, what's more reliable than God? What's easier to take for granted than the grace of the

Sovereign One who never lies and has promised always to take care of us?

And guess what? All those other essential, reliable things crossed off the top of the list depend on God's grace. To acknowledge that we need grace covers every essential need and every truly high-ranking, legitimate need. To acknowledge that we need grace is an act of worship toward God that cultivates humility in our own souls. To regularly name grace out loud as our greatest need, to openly celebrate our dependence on the grace of God at every moment and in every way, is to acknowledge to ourselves and others that all good things come through grace.

But that's not usually what happens, is it? Here is what usually happens. When I forget what my true and essential need really is, I will name things as needs that are not really needs and then invest my life in anxious pursuit of them. Subtly, these things begin to exercise control over the way I think about myself and my life. Subtly, desire for these things begins to shape the way I invest my time, energy, and money. Subtly, these things become my reason for making the decisions I make. Subtly, these things become the lens through which I evaluate my life. Subtly, I begin to look to these things for my happiness and my inner sense of well-being.

Somewhere, somehow, I have forgotten who I am. Somehow, I have let go of God's gift of grace. Somehow, walking with God has not produced in me a deeper sense of need, but just the opposite. I am smug and self-assured and because of that I am not only content to play with the box, but my life is now controlled by a replacement set of needs and along with it a replacement set of desires, hopes, dreams, and daily pursuits. My life is no longer centered on celebrating the gift I have been given. I no longer wake up in the morning with a deep sense of privilege that I have been given the one thing that everyone living in this broken-down house deeply needs: grace. Grace is no longer the paradigm for my living. Yes, I am a Christian, but I no longer celebrate daily the precious gift of grace that is the stunning glory of my life.

Sure, there will be Sunday mornings when I remember. It may take me until the fourth verse of "Amazing Grace," but for a brief moment I will remember. Or maybe in my small group, as we study the Lord's Prayer, there will be an instant of recognition. Maybe I'll learn about the divorce of a friend and for a moment I'll remember what I have been given. But those moments are fleeting, and because they are fleeting, my life isn't actually driven anymore by the purposes of the Kingdom of God. No, it is driven by visions of another kingdom.

You see, life always involves worship. Our lives revolve around the thing that has captured our attention and desire. We make continual offerings to it, sacrifices of time and energy and focus and resources, celebrating and holding up this thing to which we have ascribed such life-dominating value. This is true no matter what it is we worship: career or wealth or comfort or entertainment or reputation or relationships or self-protection . . . or Christ. Whatever it is, we celebrate it.

When you lose your sense of gratitude for your acceptance into God's Kingdom, you will lose your zeal for the work of that Kingdom. And you will live in daily pursuit and daily celebration of the purposes of some other kingdom.

What Does It Look Like to Celebrate?

So maybe the question should be, "How do I get that celebration of God's Kingdom back again?" I think the answer is found in the beginning of Psalm 122:1–2. "I rejoiced with those who said to me, 'Let us go to the house of the Lord.' Our feet are standing in your gates, O Jerusalem."

Envision the scene here as David speaks for the average Israelite. A farmer and his family are planning their pilgrimage to Jerusalem. They are brimming with excitement as they make their plans and preparations. They are actually going to the tabernacle where God dwells, and they can't believe it! They are enjoying the same kind of excited anticipation that a family would experience as they prepare to go on a particularly wonderful vacation. They are imagining the sights and sounds. They are feeling very privileged that they could make such a trip. Their hearts are not just excited *about* worship. No, their hearts are filled *with* worship already. They are recounting and remembering all that God has done for them to make this pilgrimage possible. The very thought of being in the presence of God absolutely thrills them, even as it fills them with holy fear. They have not even begun the trip yet and already their hearts are overflowing with joy.

The second sentence, "Our feet are standing in your gates, O Jerusalem," advances the scene. Now the pilgrims are actually inside the walls of the holy city. They simply cannot believe they are there, and are repeating to themselves, *I'm inside the gates. I'm inside the gates. I'm really inside the gates!* It is almost impossible for them to take it in. They are having trouble grasping that it is really true. What are these Israelites doing? They are celebrating the amazing grace of a sovereign Redeemer.

It's like us waking up in the morning and saying, *I'm redeemed. I'm redeemed. I'm redeemed. I can't believe that I am one of God's children! I can't believe that God has placed his love on me. No, my life isn't always easy, but I'm redeemed. No, the relationships with people around me don't always work the way they should, but I'm redeemed. Yes, I live in a world that is broken and does not operate as intended, but I'm redeemed. Yes, I face disappointment and suffering, but I'm redeemed. I can't believe it, I am one of God's children!*

Like David and all those he speaks for in Psalm 122, we cannot—we must not—let grace become commonplace to us. We cannot let ourselves forget the awesome privilege of being God's children; a privilege we could never have earned, deserved, or achieved on our own. We must keep in view that we are the recipients of daily grace and will never outgrow our need of what grace alone is able to provide. We must remind ourselves that because of that grace, obedience is a privilege, worship is a privilege, sacrifice is a privilege, and ministry is a privilege. The fact that we would ever choose to do any of these things is a sure sign of the transforming grace of God operating in our hearts. Apart from God's gift of grace I would make up my own laws, I would worship the creation, I would sacrifice only for what would bring me personal comfort and pleasure, and I would seek to be served rather than looking for ways to serve others.

We cannot let ourselves grow complacent. We cannot be comfortable with being forgetful. We cannot let worship decay into a weekly participation in a service. At that point, church attendance becomes mere religious routine rather than an expression of heartfelt worship of God. But when we celebrate grace in our hearts and allow ourselves to be gripped by the amazing privilege of being God's children, we go to a service of worship *because we are already worshiping*. It is the difference between passive and active, between absorbing and participating, between a focus on self and a focus on the One who came to save us from ourselves.

Apart from Christ, there simply is nothing else in life that is remotely worthy of this kind of celebration and adoration. Accomplishing the ultimate in business success, completing the most amazing physical achievement, gaining fantastic riches, attaining world power, receiving the highest honor in the eyes of others, seeing the most beautiful thing human eyes could ever see, consuming the most exotically delicious food ever prepared, becoming the wisest person on earth, or being loved by another human being in the most beautiful way ever—none of these things would be half as worthy of the celebration that should fill our hearts at the stunning recognition that by his grace, the love of God has actually been placed on us forever.

As the book of Ecclesiastes so vividly portrays, and as Philippians 3:8–11 powerfully affirms, all these other things seem vain and empty, fleeting and temporary when placed next to the surpassing greatness of knowing God.

The Battle of Celebration

Nevertheless, there is a sad truth that will follow us as long as we live in these bodies: *Celebration is war.* The worship of God doesn't come naturally to sinners like you and me. The eyes of our hearts are easily seduced by the touch-and-taste, sight-and-sound pleasures of the creation. It doesn't take long for us to imagine that perhaps life really can be found apart from Christ. And as we began to entertain those thoughts, it is a short journey from being attracted to being hooked. It is very easy to name yourself a worshiper of the Creator God, while having a life shaped by worship of and service to the creation. Even when we do get it right and place at the center the grace that alone is worthy of our celebration, we soon become desensitized to how astonishing it is. We do the unthinkable: we take grace for granted and stop celebrating the one thing in life that should amaze us for eternity.

So, we have to be good soldiers. We have to be committed to fighting for our hearts. We have to remind ourselves *daily* how quickly we get distracted, seduced, and hooked. We have to recall *daily* just how deep and pervasive our need for grace is. We have to meditate *daily* on the new identity and the new potential we have been given as children of grace. We need to warn ourselves again and again against disappointment and the danger of looking for life where life cannot be found. We have to ask ourselves what other things compete for our hearts, what other things challenge the role that the celebration of grace must have in shaping and directing the way we live. We must examine ourselves, asking if we really are worshipers of God or, instead, people who have inserted episodic, passive experiences of worship into our weekly schedule. We need to surround ourselves with other celebrants of grace and invite them to encourage and stimulate us to celebrate as well. We need to do everything we can to pass this deep and joyful sense of awe down to the next generation. We need to be like overflowing glasses of worship, making it impossible to be near us without getting wet! We need to find joy in fighting the fight. We need to understand that celebration is war.

What does this war of celebration have to do with living productively in the broken-down house? Permit me to explain in a step-by-step way.

- When you face how deep your need of God's love is, you will celebrate grace.
- When you celebrate grace, you will come to love the King of Grace more deeply.
- When you love the King of Grace more deeply, you will get excited about the work of his Kingdom of Grace.
- When you get excited about the work of the Kingdom of Grace, zeal for this Kingdom will color the way you respond to the situations and relationships you face as you live in the broken-down house.
- And as you live with eyes that see the work of God's Kingdom of Grace and a heart that loves it, you will give grace to those around you. In so doing, you will live more productively than you ever have before in the place where God has put you.

So, are you a celebrant? Has your life taken on a joy and a focus that would not be possible any other way? Or has the truly awesome become merely commonplace? Has the search for physical satisfaction consumed you more than the celebration of the spiritual realities that should now define you? Has remembrance decayed into forgetfulness? Have you lost your first love? If, so, confess your forgetfulness.

Seek God's help for your distractibility. Commit yourself to a life of celebration, knowing that this includes being a soldier in the ongoing war for your own heart. And remember that you are not alone; there is daily grace for every one of those battles.

Now, isn't that worth celebrating?

My Calling

Brief moments of
Kingdom consciousness
followed by
days and days
of self-sovereignty
and self-interest.
I give
so little of me
yet I have received
so much of You.
I treat ministry
like a big
giant step
out of what is mine
into
what is yours.
Yet
there is no
mine and yours.
You have
purchased me
with your blood.
All that I have
and
all that I am
belongs to you
for Your keeping
for Your using
for Your Kingdom
for Your glory.
All that I am
wherever I am
whatever the time
used in service of you.
This is my calling
this is Your will.

15

Minister Everywhere

*T*im had his life organized into neat little categories—work, family, church, friendships, leisure—and he was careful to give proper attention to each one. He talked a lot about "biblical balance" and "godly priorities," and it's true that even with all the success Tim had achieved in his career, he had never let work dominate his life. Family and church both figured prominently in his schedule. Every summer, for example, there was a well-planned family vacation, Tim was on regular rotation for teaching Sunday school, and he and Jody, his wife, had been on several short-term missions trips. From a distance, Tim's life seemed to be in great shape. But the closer you got, the more misshapen it appeared.

For all of Tim's outward commitment to his family, his wife and children weren't benefiting. Yes, they were right there in his calendar. Yet Jody didn't feel particularly close to her husband, an admission that was painful for her to make even to herself. Tim's kids sometimes felt like they had become part of their father's latest project; they knew how easily he could become irritated when they messed up his agenda. Up close, Tim's church life didn't look too good, either. Yes, each year included three or four defined periods of ministry. But in between, Tim's involvement with his church was reduced to attending the Sunday service.

Underlying all this was a fundamental and rather common misunderstanding. Tim did not comprehend ministry from a biblical perspective, either its nature or its scope. To him, ministry was defined by the programs and schedule of his local church. Therefore, Tim understood ministry to be episodic. It was something performed in limited pockets of time under specific circumstances to specific people for specific purposes. It was ministry on a schedule. So Tim would step out of his life into a moment of ministry and then step back out of ministry into his life. Tim had built a wall between his life and the very concept of ministry. He did not see life as ministry and he did not see ministry as something woven into daily life. Not surprisingly, Tim's approach to ministry was not working well.

Seeing Ministry for What It Is

As we begin to approach the end of this book, you will notice me once again reaching back into earlier chapters to bring forward some key ideas. This repetition is intentional. You and I are not machines. We are not computers that can instantly do new things and behave in new ways as soon as some fresh code is plugged into our memories. If you and I did not need repetition in order to learn or even to stay on course, we could read the Bible once and instantly come to full spiritual maturity. But that's just not the way it works. We learn things, especially spiritual things, at different depths and levels. Everyone who has been a Christian for more than a short period of time has had the experience of receiving fresh illumination from a passage of Scripture that may have been read dozens or even hundreds of times. So, now that we have looked further into what it means to seek to live productively in this broken-down house of a world, several points made earlier in the book ought to be revisited. With that in mind, let's consider two perspectives that challenge some assumptions Christians often have about ministry.

Life in the Fallen World Requires Ministry All the Time

Think about this: If you are living in a broken world that is not functioning as designed, and if you are living as a sinner among sinners, then there is no situation, location, or relationship where ministry is not required. You are constantly confronted with spiritual need of some kind. Therefore, it simply cannot work to define ministry as something your church leaders design, program, and schedule.

In biblical terms, ministry is not about a time or place. It is a heartfelt willingness to respond to the spiritual need that God puts in my path, *any*time, *any*place. This certainly includes participation in what my church schedules, but it must be far more. I must view every dimension of my life as a forum for ministry. Marriage is ministry. Parenting is ministry. Friendship is ministry. Living with neighbors is ministry. Work is ministry. Life is ministry.

Let's take marriage for an example. I am convinced that one reason so many Christian marriages get into difficulty is because the man and woman do not live with a ministry mentality. Underlying this is a failure of basic theology, and one manifestation of this failure is—as I mentioned earlier in this book—that they have married with unrealistic expectations. It is amazing to me how often I have counseled couples who seem shocked to discover that they have each married a sinner! They cannot imagine that the wonderful person they married has actually been selfish, or had an Oh-poor-me day, or kept a record of wrongs, or argued to be right, or been susceptible to temptation, or not been delighted at every opportunity to serve, or been lazy, or gone through times of distance from God, or wanted to be left alone, or prized personal ease more than marital unity. And why do we have these unrealistic expectations? Because we haven't taken seriously what Scripture says about who we are and where we are living.

What is a biblical view of marriage? Let me summarize it for you. Marriage involves a flawed person, in a comprehensive and interdependent love relationship with another flawed person, in the middle of a fallen world, but with a faithful God. Because this is the unchangeable reality of every marriage, there is not a day in any marriage where ministry is not required. The person you are living with is in the process of being restored. Your spouse is not yet the person God created him or her to be in this life. By his grace, God has drafted you into his service and called you to be a tool of restoration in the life of your spouse.

Or consider parenting. It amazes me how often parents are actually irritated at the amount of parenting their children seem to need! Many parents put great effort into systems that are supposed to reduce the parenting load by one means or another. But if you live in denial of the fact that parenting is about ministry, it will set you up for all kinds of problems. Vacations are a case in point.

Imagine going on a family vacation without realizing that life and ministry are one. Instead, you see vacation as an opportunity to separate yourself from the normal routine and duties of daily life. The flaw in that logic is pretty simple. If you brought sinners in the car with you, then you've brought ministry, too. So when you're down the road all of about three miles, and already your children are arguing about who is intruding into whose personal space, you can't believe it. You tell them, none too politely, that you feel like turning around and going home. You tell them you're not paying all this money just so they can do in a different and much more expensive location all the same despicable things they do at home. Your voice gets louder as you become more irritated. It doesn't seem like a vacation moment to anyone.

What's gone wrong? You have forgotten to live with a ministry mentality. A ministry mentality changes your perspective on life. It tells you that every time your eyes see or your ears hear the sin and weakness of your children, it is an act of God's grace—always grace. God loves your children and has put them in a family of faith: your family. In his restorative zeal, he will expose their sin to you so that you can be his tool of rescue and redemption for them. Ever intent on his mission, he will again and again expose their need to you. And he won't wait for a convenient opening in your schedule.

This side of eternity, healthy relationships are healthy because the people living in those relationships approach them with a ministry mentality. You never wake up to a world that has been freed from the Fall, and you never spend time with people who have escaped the curse of sin. Because of this, ministry is not something you can relegate to an area of your life or a formal slot on your schedule. No, you and I must enter each situation of life with a ministry mentality.

When I divide my existence into two separate parts—"ministry" and "my life"—guess which one gets the short end of the stick? Guess which one has to get by on my leftover time, my leftover energy, my leftover finances, and my leftover passion? If I see ministry as something that I do when I step out of my life—that is, when the church has programmed and scheduled some form of ministry for me—then the vast majority of my life is mine for the using. But Scripture teaches the reverse of those priorities. It challenges me with the reality that nothing I am or have belongs to me. I do not have a life divided into God's part and my part. It's all "God's part," the whole thing. He purchased it at the cross, when he redeemed me from a life of hopelessness on earth and eternity in hell. My life does not belong to me in any way, shape, or form. God owns me and everything my life contains.

Even something as gritty and personal as my sex life cannot be viewed as mine. My sex life does not belong to me because

I don't belong to me. I am called to a ministry mentality even in the area of sex. I am called to "glorify God" with the way I use my body sexually. The apostle Paul reveals the ownership of God over his redeemed to be utterly comprehensive, including even sexuality and sexual sin. "You are not your own, for you were bought with a price. So glorify God in your body" (1 Corinthians 6:20 ESV).

So, no part of my life belongs to me, not even the most intimate area. There is no location, situation, relationship, or dimension of my life that belongs to me. Everything I have and everything I am belongs to the Lord. It is all his for the using.

This means that I have been brought into relationship with God not only so that I could be rescued from myself, but so that I may be part of God's rescue of others. My life exists for his purposes. I was given life and breath to help maximize the glory of Another. This is why life is ministry.

We Serve a Dissatisfied Redeemer

If all of life is bound up with ministry, we need to approach life with the same perspective as the One on whose behalf we minister. As I trust you've noticed, the ongoing dissatisfaction of our Redeemer is a theme of this whole book. This God whom we serve will not quit, will not rest, will not relent until sin has finally been defeated and we are living in peace, righteousness, and justice forever. The ultimate completion of this must await the Lord's return, but in the meantime there is real work being done and real progress being made, as every life and every situation in creation is moving in the direction of Christ's final victory. God is committed to producing in every one of his children on earth greater peace, greater love, greater justice, greater deliverance from temptation, and greater freedom from sin. I'll say it again: he will not rest until every microbe of sin has been eradicated from every cell of the hearts of every one of his children. Revelation 21:5 (ESV)

196

captures God's zeal with these words, "Behold, I am making all things new."

God cannot and will not be satisfied with his work of redemption as long as the physical world suffers the effects of sin. God will not rest as long as government is corrupt and unjust. He will not rest while families are still shattered, and people made in his image are still broken by sin. He will not rest as long as poverty and disease exist. He will not rest as long as falsehood competes with truth for the hearts of people. He will not rest as long as there is an enemy who still seduces people with plausible lies. He will not rest until everything is exactly as it was meant to be when he set his powerful hands to create it. God never stops working in opposition to sin and the effects of the Fall, and his working is always effective.

If God is dissatisfied, then I should be as well. Yet I am persuaded that our problem is not that we are dissatisfied, but that we are all too easily *satisfied*. We are easily satisfied with an externalistic and episodic Christianity that lives most fully on Sunday morning. We are easily satisfied with an approach to theological knowledge and biblical literacy that does not reshape and redefine how we live. We easily are satisfied with marriages that are more marital détente than they are pictures of one-flesh unity. We are easily satisfied with raising children who learn to jump through our behavioral hoops, but don't really have hearts for God. We are easily satisfied having casual relationships with neighbors who live in darkness and desperately need to see the Light of Life. We are all too content to lower our standards enough to participate in entertainment that is increasingly perverse in its depiction of life.

We can actually get to the place, in our busyness and selfishness, where we just don't care anymore. We walk each day through a terribly broken world that no longer moves us, whose cries we no longer hear. We want life to be regular, predictable, comfortable, and controllable, and as long as it is, we are satisfied enough to be complacent. In our complacency, we are pleased in places and situations where God is not pleased, and passive in places where God is active and calling us to be active as well.

Our ability to be satisfied when we ought to be dissatisfied reveals that we see our lives as belonging to us. We are satisfied because life is giving us what we want. When it doesn't, we try to whip the people and situations around us into shape so they more fully conform to our will. Does this sound harsh to you? Let's go back to the example of marriage.

I think that quite often, even among Christians, a man or a woman is attracted to someone of the opposite sex, not out of love for that person, but out of love for oneself. A woman may be attracted to a man because she thinks he may be the missing puzzle piece to the dream she has for her life. The attraction he holds for her, and the delight he brings her, feels like love in her heart for him, when it really isn't. Mostly she loves herself, and what excites her about this man is that he may be able to give her what she wants.

The man may be doing essentially the same thing. He is not attracted to this woman primarily because he loves her, but because he loves himself. This woman is his ticket to the good life. His emotions toward her feel like love, but they aren't.

Imagine that this man and woman get married (and honestly, this happens all the time). They think they love one another, but in the biblical sense they really don't. What they love is what the other person appears to offer them. What they have actually married is their dream. In an act of narcissism, they have made a lifelong vow to an aspect of themselves.

Predictably, the bliss doesn't last very long, because marriage only works well when it is fueled by self-sacrificing, ministry-committed love. Within weeks or months the newly-weds are responding to one another with low-grade irritation and impatience. A little longer and irritation has degenerated into full-blown anger. She cries, "This man doesn't love me!" He yells, "This woman does not respect me!"

What has happened is inevitable, a direct result of the collision of two worlds built on self-focused dreams. This man and woman did not marry out of sacrificial love. Sadly and unbeknownst to them, their relationship has been fueled by the inverted passion of self-love. Now they are hurt and discouraged, but not because the other person has broken the laws of God's Kingdom. No, the wife is hurt because the husband broke the rules of her kingdom, and the husband is hurt because the wife broke the rules of his. As they finally begin to glimpse the true nature of the problem, they are overwhelmed with how much personal sacrifice will be needed to make this marriage into what it was intended to be. They are overwhelmed to recognize, although they may not be able to state it this way, that healthy relationships must be based on a ministry mentality.

We are called to share our Redeemer's dissatisfaction, but I am afraid that often we don't. I am afraid that one of the results of sin in all of our hearts is a perverse ability to be satisfied when we should not be. We all learn in some way to be okay with things that are not okay. When this happens, we quit caring. And when we quit caring, we stop living with a ministry mentality.

A Better Way

As long as we are still living in the broken-down house, we must constantly remind ourselves that *life is ministry and ministry is life*. We must buy into the ministry paradigm that is all over the New Testament. (See Ephesians 4:1–16, 25–29.) It is what I have called elsewhere God's *total involvement* model of ministry, that is, *all of God's people, all of the time*.

No teaching gets at this more powerfully than these verses from Christ's Sermon on the Mount:

"You are the salt of the earth. But if the salt loses its saltiness, how can it be made salty again? It is no longer good for anything, except to be thrown out and trampled by men. You are the light of the world. A city on a hill cannot be hidden. Neither do people light a lamp and put it under a bowl. Instead they put it on its stand, and it gives light to everyone in the house. In the same way, let your light shine before men, that they may see your good deeds and praise your Father in heaven."

—Matthew 5:13–16

What Christ does here is amazing. He who called himself the Light of the World (John 8:12) assigns to us the same name! What is he saying? He is telling us that our mission here is to reflect his light wherever darkness exists. Now think about this. There is never a day that you are not in contact with darkness in some form. Maybe it is the darkness of your child's rebellion. Maybe it is the darkness of a community injustice. Maybe it is the darkness of the materialism all around you, or your marital difficulties, or the solitude and alienation of someone in your neighborhood. Maybe it is the darkness of the whininess and self-focus that complicates the relationships around you. Maybe it is the darkness of the falsehoods that grip the culture you live in. Somehow, some way, at street level, you are in contact with darkness every day.

How are you called to respond? You must not be content with avoiding the darkness. You must not be content with surviving the darkness. You are called to shine light *into* the darkness. Jesus is essentially saying, "You have been lit by the light of my grace and truth. Now go shine!" The passage calls us to consider how nonsensical it would be to light a lamp and then cover it. Truly, to have a light, yet obscure it so it lights nothing, simply makes no sense.

That darkness is all around us, everywhere we go. Yet to each of these places we carry with us the light of transforming grace. That which has been so tragically darkened by sin can be illuminated by the Light of the World who dwells within us. Because of this, I can live excited by my new-found ministry potential. I can live looking for opportunities to shine, that I might be part of what God is doing in the places where he has put me. I can begin to be motivated by the high calling I have been given. I can be justifiably amazed that God would choose me to be part of the most important work in the universe—the redemption of the lost.

How could it be that God would place his name on me? How could it be that he would pick me up in his hands and use me as a tool of renewal, restoration, and redemption? No matter how much worldly success I achieve, no matter how much wealth I acquire, no matter how much honor in the eyes of others I am given, and no matter how many wonderful things I experience, there is nothing that could ever compete or compare with the surpassing honor of knowing God and being chosen to be part of what he is doing on earth.

Vision, Commitment, Training

What does this look like, in practical terms, for how I approach daily living? It means I must commit myself to three things: *vision*, *commitment*, and *training*.

I must daily pray that God would make me a person of *vision*. With the eyes of my heart, I need to be able to see myself from a biblical perspective. I need to keep in view every day that, entirely because of what God has done in me, I really am the light of the world. I really have been called to be the salt of the earth. This vision of my identity should shape the way I respond to everything I encounter, every day.

In addition, I must daily pray that as I go out into the world that I would see—really see. It is so easy to be distracted by busyness and self-interest. It is so easy to live with head down and eyes closed. It is so easy to look at profound need and not see it. It is so easy to stare ministry opportunities in the face and not notice them. It is so easy to look at life through the lens of personal desire, agenda, feelings, needs, or purpose. We need God's help to look at life through a different lens— the lens of his redemptive zeal for this broken world, and our calling to live and minister out of that zeal.

Living a ministry lifestyle also means *commitment*. I have to commit myself to structuring my life so that ministry is actually possible. If I am a parent, I am called to minister to my children. This means I will do more than just figure out ways to get them to obey me. I will invest the time and energy necessary to get at issues of the heart so that I might function as an instrument of heart change in their lives. If I am married, I am called to minister to my spouse. This will mean investing in regular time with my spouse so we can develop a relationship of knowledge, tenderness, and love—the kind of relationship that promotes honest communication and, therefore, God's work of personal change. As a friend, I am called to minister to my friends. This means not settling for a network of permanently casual relationships, but developing a mature and knowledgeable circle of relationships that functions as a workroom for the Redeemer. As a member of the body of Christ, this commitment means not waiting for the church to schedule and program my life of ministry. It means looking at my life with a ministry lens, living with a ministry mentality.

Perhaps this example will help. Jack and Sally are members of a very good church. Their lives are woven into wonderful fellowship relationships and they are involved in everyday and church-sponsored ministries. Both Jack and Sally would say they have grown significantly through the ministry of their small group and circle of friends. They would also say they have been excited at the ministry opportunities God has opened up in their community. Then one day, Jack is unexpectedly approached by the president of his company and asked if he would be willing to move to another city to lead the opening of a new division. In many ways it is the career opportunity of Jack's dreams. Not only would he be in charge and able to exercise his creative leadership gifts as never before, he would get a significant raise. At first it seems like an easy decision.

But as Jack and Sally begin to consider moving, they immediately think of the amazing group of friends God has provided for them and how these people have been such a significant part of their spiritual growth (and vice versa). Then they think of the people in their neighborhood who they are actively ministering to. They think of Mrs. Gretsch, who they know will panic without Sally's daily visits. They think of Tom and Sue, who are just beginning to trust them enough to open up. They think of the families they have gotten to know through the Little League and the summer picnics that they have held at their house at the end of each season. Sally thinks of the small Bible study she began a year ago that only now seems to be catching on. Jack thinks of the men's small group he attends and his work as a deacon.

The more they think about it, the less attractive the career opportunity looks. They know that to replicate, in a new place, the ministries they are involved in and receiving from would take a decade. So they decide to be content with the present situation and celebrate the good things God has given them and is daily calling them to. Jack turns down the promotion.

There is a third thing that living with a ministry mentality requires: *training*. If I really do see ministry as *my* calling and not just the calling of the paid professionals in my church, I will get serious about doing anything I can to hone my ministry understanding and skill. I will be a committed student of the Word of God. I will want to take advantage of any Sunday school class, seminar, workshop, or book that can help me think more practically about what it actually looks like to function as a tool for change in the hands of a powerful and gracious Redeemer.

Remember, in this broken-down house that we all live in, every room of life is at the same time a forum for ministry. You will never face a day that is not filled with ministry need and opportunity. The questions are, Are your eyes open to the need, and Are you capturing the God-given opportunities?

Legacy

It's impossible not to
somehow
someway.
I will leave a
trail
behind me.
I will leave
footprints
for others to
follow.
Footprints of
relationships
values
character
worldview
worship.
Footprints
of some kind of
glory.
May my trail point
others
to the glory
that can only be found in
You.

16

Examine Your Legacy

As I was thinking about how to conclude a book on living productively in a fallen world, it hit me that as Christians we believe life has consequences. We really do believe that this world—this entire creation—is ordered and not random. We believe that because everything we see is the intentional, creative product of a holy God, morality actually matters. We believe in right and wrong, in good and bad, and in true and false. We believe in a God who created us for his purpose and has called for us to live in a certain way. We do not believe in an open universe where you can live any way you want, enjoying success and suffering no consequences.

Because we believe these things, we see every choice, word, and action as having meaning and producing a result. We really do believe that every day we plant seeds and every day we harvest what we have planted in the past. We believe in the sanctity of choices and the power of decisions. We believe that we all invest our lives in some way and that every life investment has some kind of return.

Maybe the best way to talk about this is to encourage you to stop reading for a moment. Not right now—after the next paragraph. Let me urge you to take thirty seconds to examine the investments you are making now and the return they are likely to leave behind. You can do that by considering the following questions:

What have you poured your time and energy into *today*? What have you invested in so far *this week*? This *month*? This *year*? Where have your efforts gone, and what do you think will come of them?

OK, thirty seconds . . .

Jot some notes in the margins of this book if you want to. Because no matter who you are, no matter what your situation, and no matter what your answers are, there is definitely one thing that you have been doing, consciously or otherwise. You have been building your legacy.

A legacy isn't optional. It's impossible not to leave one. Every day, every choice, every moment, you build your own legacy, little by little. This legacy is what you leave behind when you die, the inheritance you pass along to others. Sometimes we think of it as primarily financial, an inheritance of personal wealth. There is much talk of how leaders in politics, business, the arts, and other areas leave a legacy of accomplishments and influence, whether good or bad. But the most important kind of legacy, and the kind we want to focus on here, is a spiritual legacy.

A Good Way to Live Badly

Bob was successful, and he knew how to make others successful. He firmly believed that success is not something you are given, but something you build. Yet he was convinced that most people had never learned to "be successful," and that drove him crazy. He felt that most people were too lazy, that they set the bar way too low for themselves ever to truly succeed.

Even as a teenager, Bob had recognized that education is an important part of success, so he took his schooling seriously and did well. After college, his career was a steady climb up the ladder of achievement. Bob became wealthy and powerful. He was obsessed with success and determined that everyone around him be successful as well. This brought some positive results in his business, but did not have quite the same effect in his family.

Although Bob was a Christian, his home was more like a military boot camp than a place of grace. Bob's children lived with an endless cycle of demands, waking up every morning to run the drills of their father's expectations. There was little rest or leisure, little approval or encouragement, and a sense of intimidation often swept through the house like a cold fog. Yes, there were times of laughter and celebration, but these were brief and infrequent. Sure, there was love in Bob's home, but it was not what you would call a loving home. It was more like taking a never-ending exam. To live in Bob's home was to be taught by example that relationships take a back seat to personal achievement.

Even worse, to live in Bob's home was to be taught by example that worship of God is an important religious duty, but really nothing more. Bob taught his children to be serious about going to church and understanding a few basic points of doctrine. But when it came to teaching them what it means to worship God in everything you do, he failed completely.

Bob didn't lead his children in worship or celebration of God. He didn't point his children to the sight-and-sound display of the glory of God that surrounded them. He didn't discuss the gifts, skills, and achievements of his children in terms of the plan and purposes of the Kingdom of God. He didn't teach his children to examine their motives, to critique their thoughts, or to evaluate what they really were living for.

If you lived within Bob's sphere of influence, life was not daily connected to the knowledge of God, the worship of God, or what it means to love God. Spiritual things, the wonder of eternity, and the ongoing cosmic struggle for the thoughts and motives of the heart were almost never discussed. Bob's was a family where the reality of sin's self-focus and the gift of God's transforming grace were simply not matters of serious consideration. Bob talked about the importance of faith in Christ, but in the face of how he lived and ran his home, these were empty words.

Rather than passing along a legacy of celebrating and worshiping God, Bob had schooled his children in idolatry. He had taught them how to build their own little kingdom, and how to live in it like a little king. He had taught them to attach their identity, meaning, purpose, and inner sense of well-being not to God, but to personal achievement. In the final analysis, Bob actually taught his children to worship a false god, the god of personal power and success.

As a result, Bob's children did not think of God as standing in the center of their universe. Having thoroughly absorbed the message that material things are more valuable than spiritual things, they grew up and became very successful— in exactly the ways Bob had defined success for them. Not surprisingly, they had even less time for God than Bob did. Each one attended a church. Each one claimed faith in God. They did not become angry atheists or bored agnostics. But for them, the vague image of a Sunday-only God had grown even fainter, even less interesting, and even less worthy of close attention.

A Strong Spiritual Legacy Is Always Intentional

Whether you are a parent or not, you will inevitably leave something to those who come behind you. What will your spiritual legacy be? What are you building? What of your life will remain when you go to be with Christ?

Leaving a strong, God-glorifying spiritual legacy never happens by accident; it is never the path of least resistance. It is intentional and begins with understanding how such a legacy can be formed. Let me delineate for you some principles that help create the sort of legacy each one of God's children should want to leave for those who follow.

Relationships Are Central to God's Purpose for You

Did you know that Jesus gave us a brief, clear definition of what makes for a successful life?

> Hearing that Jesus had silenced the Sadducees, the Pharisees got together. One of them, an expert in the law, tested him with this question: "Teacher, which is the greatest commandment in the Law?" Jesus replied: "'Love the Lord your God with all your heart and with all your soul and with all your mind.' This is the first and greatest commandment. And the second is like it: 'Love your neighbor as yourself.' All the Law and the Prophets hang on these two commandments."
>
> —Matthew 22:34–39

I don't think it's too strong to say that, right here, Jesus identified two things that must appear in any life that can truly be called successful. For Jesus, a life invested as God designed it has at its core strong relationships: living for God above all else and loving my neighbor as myself.

Or consider Paul's surprising words in Galatians 5:13–14. "You, my brothers, were called to be free. But do not use your freedom to indulge the sinful nature; rather, serve one another in love. The entire law is summed up in a single command: 'Love your neighbor as yourself.'"

A single command? Isn't Paul missing the vital first half of Jesus' two-part definition? No, it's more that he is folding them together, for Paul knows that only people who love God above all else are even capable of loving their neighbors as themselves. When I don't love you as I love myself, it's because I don't love God enough.

Consider also what John says in 1 John 4:7–12, 16–21:

Dear friends, let us love one another, for love comes from God. Everyone who loves has been born of God and knows God. Whoever does not love does not know God, because God is love. This is how God showed his love among us: He sent his one and only Son into the world that we might live through him. This is love: not that we loved God, but that he loved us and sent his Son as an atoning sacrifice for our sins. Dear friends, since God so loved us, we also ought to love one another. No one has ever seen God; but if we love one another, God lives in us and his love is made complete in us . . . .

And so we know and rely on the love God has for us.

God is love. Whoever lives in love lives in God, and God in him. In this way, love is made complete among us so that we will have confidence on the day of judgment, because in this world we are like him. There is no fear in love. But perfect love drives out fear, because fear has to do with punishment. The one who fears is not made perfect in love.

We love because he first loved us. If anyone says, "I love God," yet hates his brother, he is a liar. For anyone who does not love his brother, whom he has seen, cannot love God, whom he has not seen. And he has given us this command: Whoever loves God must also love his brother.

Here, at the end of this passage, John makes more explicit what Paul treated as assumed: loving God is a prerequisite to loving others biblically. These two kinds of love are meant to go together. John essentially says that if you want to know the true quality of your relationship with God, don't look at your theological knowledge, biblical literacy, church involvement, etc. (although all these are very important). Instead, you should look at the quality of the relationships you have with those whom you live closest to. It is impossible truly to love God and not live lovingly with the people God has placed you near.

Who of us is not convicted by John's words? I was sitting with my family recently, listening to my adult children participate in one of those gloriously chaotic multiple conversations, when my mind wandered. Suddenly I began to remember other conversations; ones not so wise or pleasant or gracious. A stab of pain traveled through my heart as I recalled moments of irritation, impatience, and criticism. By God's grace, I do think our home has largely been a place of love. Nevertheless, there have been far too many moments that I now regret.

I don't wallow in my guilt, because I believe in the glory of God's forgiveness through Christ Jesus. All the same, I think it is wholesome for us to look back, to remember, and to assess the degree to which we have loved others as we have been loved. A biblically rich spiritual legacy will always place a high value on living in loving community with others. This life of love is an expression of a heart of love, not just for people, but for the God who created them and placed them in our lives.

The Most Valuable Treasures Are Spiritual

What should you want to leave behind as your spiritual legacy? Two things will pretty much cover it: a sense of what is truly worth living for, and an awareness of how seductive and deceptive the physical pleasures of the created world can be. Such pleasures are God-given and certainly have their place. But as Christ's teaching in Matthew 6:19–34 captures so powerfully, these must not be what we live for.

"Do not store up for yourselves treasures on earth, where moth and rust destroy, and where thieves break in and steal. But store up for yourselves treasures in heaven, where moth and rust do not destroy, and where thieves do not break in and steal. For where your treasure is, there your heart will be also.

"The eye is the lamp of the body. If your eyes are good, your whole body will be full of light. But if your eyes are bad, your whole body will be full of darkness. If then the light within you is darkness, how great is that darkness!

"No one can serve two masters. Either he will hate the one and love the other, or he will be devoted to the one and despise the other. You cannot serve both God and Money.

211

"Therefore I tell you, do not worry about your life, what you will eat or drink; or about your body, what you will wear. Is not life more important than food, and the body more important than clothes? Look at the birds of the air; they do not sow or reap or store away in barns, and yet your heavenly Father feeds them. Are you not much more valuable than they? Who of you by worrying can add a single hour to his life?

"And why do you worry about clothes? See how the lilies of the field grow. They do not labor or spin. Yet I tell you that not even Solomon in all his splendor was dressed like one of these. If that is how God clothes the grass of the field, which is here today and tomorrow is thrown into the fire, will he not much more clothe you, O you of little faith? So do not worry, saying, 'What shall we eat?' or 'What shall we drink?' or 'What shall we wear?' For the pagans run after all these things, and your heavenly Father knows that you need them. But seek first his kingdom and his righteousness, and all these things will be given to you as well. Therefore do not worry about tomorrow, for tomorrow will worry about itself. Each day has enough trouble of its own."

A sad fact of the Fall is that sin has turned us all into materialists. Each of us fights a moment-by-moment battle to keep the physical glories of creation in their proper place in our hearts. In the passage above, Christ warns that physical treasures are temporary; compared to eternal treasures, they are fleeting and unsatisfying. Look to physical things to comfort our hearts, and we end up overweight, in debt, addicted, or all three.

You see, we are all moral bankers. Every day we make a dozen or a hundred or a thousand little mundane investments in the hope of gaining some kind of return. You may not consciously think this way, but this is what you are doing. Every person living is pursuing some kind of treasure. Your actions, reactions, and responses in any given situation or relationship represent your deposits, your attempts to secure whatever in that moment is valuable to you.

Christ's words alert us to the fact that either we are living for the physical treasures of the created world, which have a very short shelf-life, or we are living for the eternal satisfaction that can only be found in the treasures of God's Kingdom. This is why we cannot afford to live mindlessly, oblivious to the war of desire that rages in our hearts.

God's accepting grace and transforming love are eternal treasures that will never pass away. They really are the only things in life worth living for. When you live for the Kingdom of God, when God's purposes on earth become more precious and important to you than your purposes, you live for something that will never end.

As we read in Revelation the words of the celebrants on the other side, there is not a song of lament or a hymn of regret to be found. There is only an endless celebration of the grace of the Lamb. Why? Because those who sing are no longer waging a treasure war. Their values have finally been clarified, their hearts finally purified. They now know that every investment they made in the things of God was fully and completely worth it. They are satisfied, not because they got everything they wanted in this life, but because God accomplished everything he promised.

Character Trumps Achievement

We live in a world that worships at the altar of achievement and success. We typically evaluate and honor people, not by the attitude and character of their hearts, but by their home, their car, their paycheck, their vacations, or the number of people who answer to them. The Bible certainly does not denigrate success. To the contrary, it urges us to be excellent in all we do. But at every step, Scripture places moral character *above* achievement. Recall this story from 1 Samuel 16:6–7.

> When they arrived, Samuel saw Eliab and thought, "Surely the Lord's anointed stands here before the Lord." But the Lord said to Samuel, "Do not consider his appearance or his height, for I have rejected him. The Lord does not look at the things

man looks at. Man looks at the outward appearance, but the
LORD looks at the heart."

Samuel, impressed by the size and appearance of Eliab, thought
he must certainly be the future king of Israel. But it was not
so. God's evaluation of people does not rest on externals. God
has radically different criteria. He looks on the heart.

He who made us knows that what rules our hearts will
control our words and actions, and thus direct the course of
our life. So he sought a man to serve as king of Israel whose
heart belonged to God. Such a heart will have character qualities only God can produce.

Scripture portrays those qualities—and their opposites—
in passages like Galatians 5:19-26. These verses present a
clear and very helpful contrast between godly and ungodly
character.

> The acts of the sinful nature are obvious: sexual immorality,
> impurity and debauchery; idolatry and witchcraft; hatred, dis-
> cord, jealousy, fits of rage, selfish ambition, dissensions, fac-
> tions and envy; drunkenness, orgies, and the like. I warn you,
> as I did before, that those who live like this will not inherit
> the kingdom of God.
>
> But the fruit of the Spirit is love, joy, peace, patience, kind-
> ness, goodness, faithfulness, gentleness and self-control. Against
> such things there is no law. Those who belong to Christ Jesus
> have crucified the sinful nature with its passions and desires.
> Since we live by the Spirit, let us keep in step with the Spirit. Let
> us not become conceited, provoking and envying each other.

In each of our lives, this passage is meant to function as a
tool of personal insight and a spur to transformation. Each of
us suffers from a distorted view of self. As sinners, it is hard for
us to be objective and accurate in our self-assessment. During
counseling, countless people have angrily declared to me that
they were not angry, or self-righteously declared to me that
they were not self-righteous. People can be astonishingly blind

to the impact they have on others, and stone deaf to the tone of their own voice. Indeed, one of the main functions of the Bible is to help us see ourselves as we actually are.

A culture that has replaced identity in the Lord with identity in material things—the culture you and I live in every day—will always prize achievement, success, and possessions over character. In such a culture we will be so obsessed with what we want to *do* that we will have little time to consider who we should *be*. But here's the dilemma: unless we *are* what we are supposed to *be*, we cannot possibly *do* what we have been called to.

Let us leave behind us the false cultural understanding of what's important, so that this erroneous view does not become our legacy. Let us instead model and teach the importance of godly character.

Everything You Do Flows from Your Functional Worldview

Everyone is a philosopher. Everyone is a theologian. Everyone is an archeologist, digging through the mound of his existence seeking to make sense of it. Everyone is a contractor, building his life on a foundation of "truths," whether real or imagined. Everyone is a treasure hunter, searching for something valuable enough to live for.

In other words, everyone has a worldview. A worldview is like a lens through which you see life. It's a set of beliefs that forms the basis of your identity, your sense of life's meaning. It is the moral framework by which you make decisions, the value system that shapes your relationships. From it flow the assumptions that give you a measure of inner rest and well-being.

However, because we are frail creatures—human and not machines, sin-polluted mixtures of rationality and irrationality, sinners yet children of grace—we do not live with faultless consistency. This is not simply a matter of practicing one's worldview imperfectly. It's much deeper than that. In fact, everyone tends to have *two* worldviews: a confessional, professed worldview and a functional, actual worldview; the one they claim—even to themselves—and the one they really live. We may carry around a well-crafted, theologically precise, and biblically consistent worldview. But against the tug of daily living, that professed worldview does not always exercise the pull that it should. At the street level of daily life, the way we actually live reveals what we truly believe.

For example, many Christians who have the sovereignty of God as a principle element of their professed worldview still fret over their circumstances or work way too hard to establish control over things. Many Christians say they are sinners, yet stubbornly defend themselves when confronted with an area of sin in their life. Many Christians claim to believe that the most important things in life are unseen, yet they invest their time, energy, and resources in a life-long pursuit of physical pleasure and comfort.

So, for all the importance of your theological confession, your true worldview is always laid bare by the choices you make, the words you say, and the actions you take. The ultimate test is real human behavior in the real world. "Beliefs" not lived are "beliefs" that have not been truly believed. In Hebrews 11, the Bible's most extensive treatise on the nature of true faith, the writer says little about the theology of the people he mentions. He is primarily concerned with telling us what they did when the pressure was on.

How we view Scripture and handle Scripture is absolutely central to this matter of worldview. The Bible is not a book of topics. It is not a string of morality tales. It is not a compendium of theological truths. The Bible is a single, sweeping story with God's notes, a theologically annotated narrative. This grand redemptive story has been given to you and me by God to provide the lens through which we can understand our own stories and their immediate, direct connection to the story of everything that exists.

The Bible is God's helicopter view of everyday life. Every major question of human existence is asked and answered by the biblical story. A few examples:

- Is there a God, and if so, who is he?
- Who am I?
- What is the one problem underlying all my other problems, and how can it be solved?
- How can this world be so full of wonder and beauty, and at the same time so full of pain and depravity?
- Is this present life all that there is, and if there is more, how can I know where I am headed?

There is no portion of Scripture that emphasizes the importance of your worldview better than the book of Ecclesiastes. Yet it does this in a way that can be easily misunderstood. Let's look at the opening passage, then review what the book is really saying.

The words of the Teacher, son of David, king in Jerusalem:

"Meaningless! Meaningless!"
says the Teacher.
"Utterly meaningless!
Everything is meaningless."
What does man gain from all his labor
at which he toils under the sun?
Generations come and generations go,
but the earth remains forever.
The sun rises and the sun sets,
and hurries back to where it rises.
The wind blows to the south
and turns to the north;
round and round it goes,
ever returning on its course.
All streams flow into the sea,
yet the sea is never full.

To the place the streams come from,
there they return again.
All things are wearisome,
more than one can say.
The eye never has enough of seeing,
nor the ear its fill of hearing.
What has been will be again,
what has been done will be done again;
there is nothing new under the sun.
Is there anything of which one can say,
"Look! This is something new"?
It was here already, long ago;
it was here before our time.
There is no remembrance of men of old,
and even those who are yet to come
will not be remembered
by those who follow.
—Ecclesiastes 1:1–11

What is all this apparent hopelessness and meaninglessness that continues for twelve elegant, poetic chapters? Very simply, it is the worldview that we want to *leave behind us*. This book is designed to drive us to God by showing us in an artfully indirect way that there really is no hope—and here's the key phrase—*under the sun*.

Don't be confused by the refrain of "Meaningless, meaningless, everything is meaningless." The doctrines of creation and the cross really do infuse life with meaning at *every* point. Ecclesiastes is not contradicting the biblical worldview. It is an emphatic, unqualified affirmation of that view, yet stated in the negative.

The writer's purpose is to show that life simply cannot and will not make any sense, nor can it retain any purpose or achieve any meaningful goal, without the existence, character, and plan of God. The word-picture phrase "under the sun" appears in Ecclesiastes twenty-seven times, and refers to a world without God, who exists "above the sun"—that is, beyond the created order. The whole point of the book is to demonstrate all the ways in which life is meaningless when you leave God out of the picture, as if this world were self-contained and self-created.

The writer wants to depress you . . . temporarily. He wants you to respond, "No—there is, there *must* be, there *has to* be more to life than this!" He wants you to cry out for the one thing that can give meaning back to life, the one place to ground your worldview: God, his story, and what *his* purpose means for *your* purpose.

Your Life Purpose Is to Live for God's Glory

At various points in this book we have touched on the centrality of worship to everyday living. We have seen that worship is not just one activity among many for a Christian, but the foundational fact of his or her identity. I was created as a worshiper, with God as the sole intended object of my worship. Everything I do somehow, in some way, expresses worship of something or someone. I was given breath so that ideally my every thought, word, and deed might be shaped by the worship of God. Having been created as a worshiper, I am hardwired to respond to glory, of which there are only two varieties: sign glory and ultimate glory.

Sign glory is created glory—all the magnificent attributes of this beautiful and amazing world God has made. These things were created to function like signposts, pointing us to the glory of God. We must not look to them for our identity and fulfillment, and they are not worthy of our worship, because they simply were not created with the capacity to satisfy us. Their beauty is but a hint, a reflection, a foretaste of what's to come.

Ultimate glory is the glory of God himself. God's glory is the only true glory, but in this life we can bear mere glimpses and reflections of it, primarily in the form of sign glory. God's is the only glory we were made to be enthralled with, and the only glory that can ever satisfy the hunger in our hearts.

How can we leave, as the core element of our spiritual legacy, a right view of this ultimate glory? How can we gift those who follow with a knowledge of their identity as worshipers, and a knowledge that satisfaction can only ever be found in living for the glory of God? We can do no better than seek to follow the example given us in Psalm 145. No portion of God's word captures a commitment to this legacy of worship better than this psalm.

> I will exalt you, my God the King;
> I will praise your name for ever and ever.
> Every day I will praise you
> and extol your name forever and ever.
> Great is the LORD and most worthy of praise;
> his greatness no one can fathom.
> One generation will commend your works to another;
> they will tell of your mighty acts.
> They will speak of the glorious splendor of your majesty,
> and I will meditate on your wonderful works.
> They will tell of the power of your awesome works,
> and I will proclaim your great deeds.
> They will celebrate your abundant goodness
> and joyfully sing of your righteousness.
> The LORD is gracious and compassionate,
> slow to anger and rich in love.
> The LORD is good to all;
> he has compassion on all he has made.
> All you have made will praise you, O LORD;
> your saints will extol you.
> They will tell of the glory of your kingdom
> and speak of your might,
> so that all men may know of your mighty acts
> and the glorious splendor of your kingdom.
> Your kingdom is an everlasting kingdom,
> and your dominion endures through all generations.
> The LORD is faithful to all his promises
> and loving toward all he has made.

The LORD upholds all those who fall
    and lifts up all who are bowed down.
The eyes of all look to you,
    and you give them their food at the proper time.
You open your hand
    and satisfy the desires of every living thing.
The LORD is righteous in all his ways
    and loving toward all he has made.
The LORD is near to all who call on him,
    to all who call on him in truth.
He fulfills the desires of those who fear him;
    he hears their cry and saves them.
The LORD watches over all who love him,
    but all the wicked he will destroy.
My mouth will speak in praise of the LORD.
Let every creature praise his holy name
    for ever and ever.

In Psalm 145 we are presented with a legacy of awe. One devastating, tragic result of the materialism and secularism of Western culture is that it has taken from us the awe of God. Awe was meant to keep you safe, to make you humble, to motivate you to be moral, to draw you to seek the grace you so desperately need, and to convince you to live for something bigger than yourself! Awe was meant to get you up in the morning and to give you rest at night. Awe was meant to remind you that your hope is not to be found in what you achieve or possess, but is only ever to be found in the glory of the character and plan of Another.

Creation was designed, not to be the center of your awe, but to point you to its awesome Creator. The special revelation of Scripture is meant to deepen and focus your awe. The cross was meant to give you back the awe that all of us lose when we spend more time trying to be God than living in heartfelt awe of God.

I am always saddened when I see a teenager in the back of a church, slumped down in the seat, with a look that says, "I have no awe of anything that happens here." I am sad because there, at age sixteen, this young person has already lost the key ingredient of biblically productive living: awe of God.

In counseling I have heard countless recitations of men's wrongs against their wives. As I listen, I am hit again and again with the reality that these men have remaining within them no functional awe of God, his glory, or his authority. And what they do not possess they cannot possibly pass along to their children. This is why we need to examine our own hearts. Does awe live there? And this is why we need to remember that there is no better spiritual legacy, no greater blessing we could leave to others, than a bold, clear-eyed vision of the glory of God, and a heart that is both in awe of that glory and committed to live for it!

Broken-Down House, Joyful Productive Living

So, we end this book where we began.

Yes, you are living in a broken-down house. Here, you will face discouragement, danger, disappointment, and grief. There will be times when life will seem overwhelmingly hard. There will be broken-plumbing, shattered-glass moments when it seems like this world can never be and will never be restored. Sometimes you will wonder if it is all worth it.

But you can, beyond any question, live productively in this broken world. There are things worth living for and things worthy of celebration. You can, beyond any question, be one of God's tools of rescue and restoration. You can live a restoration lifestyle with the sure expectation that one day he will look into your eyes, put a tender hand on your tired shoulder, and say, "Well done, good and faithful servant." You can do these things, and know these things, because of grace.

For there is coming a day when the final triumph of God's grace will be manifested, and we will see a new heaven and a new earth. The house will be completely and perfectly restored and we will celebrate our perfected dwelling forever. Until then, however, here's what you need to remember.

There is never a situation, location, or relationship that you enter alone. Your Lord is not away somewhere and he never sleeps. He never greets your calls with a busy signal. He is never too tired or too busy to respond. He will never mock your ignorance or weakness, and he does not cruelly throw your failure in your face. He will never threaten that he is at the end of his rope with you. He will not grow weary of your inconsistencies, bored with your ambivalence, or irritated when once again you fall short.

His loving face will always be toward you and, because of the cross, you will never see the back of his head. He will meet your moment-by-moment needs—providing strength from his Spirit, wisdom from his Word, resources from the body of Christ, forgiveness that is your daily need, and deliverance from constant temptation. Even the trials he sends your way will supply what you need: the character to live for him more effectively. These are all evidences of his commitment to you, that you might be who you are supposed to be and do what he has created you to do.

This is the God of grace who calls you to resist passivity and discouragement. He calls you to fight the urge to give in or give up. He calls you to live with perseverance now and to invest wholeheartedly in what is to come. He calls you to hold firmly to the same thing believed by all the saints who have gone before us: "that he exists and that he rewards those who earnestly seek him" (Hebrews 11:6).